Language in Education: Theory and Practice

From the Classroom to the Community

A Fifteen-Year Experiment in Refugee Education

Edited by Donald A. Ranard & Margo Pfleger

A co-publication of the Center for Applied Linguistics and
Delta Systems Co., Inc.

Prepared by the Refugee Service Center and the
ERIC Clearinghouse on Languages and Linguistics

Language in Education: Theory and Practice 86

The contents of this book were developed under an agreement financed by the Bureau of Population, Refugees, and Migration, United States Department of State, but do not necessarily represent the policy of that agency and should not assume endorsement by the Federal Government.

This book was prepared for publication with funding from the Office of Educational Research and Improvement, U.S. Department of Education, under contract No. RR 93002010. The opinions expressed herein do not necessarily reflect the positions or policies of OERI or ED.

Editorial/production supervision: Jeanne Rennie
Editorial assistance: Sonia Kundert
Copyediting: Sarah Neal
Production: Sonia Kundert
Design and cover: Vincent Sagart

ISBN 0-937354-55-4

Printed in the United States of America

10 9 8 7 6 5 4 3 2 1

Library of Congress Cataloging-in-Publication Data

From the classroom to the community : a fifteen-year experiment in
    refugee education / edited by Donald A. Ranard & Margo Pfleger.
        p.   cm. -- (Language in education ; 86)
    "Prepared by the Refugee Service Center and the ERIC Clearinghouse
on Languages and Linguistics."
    Includes bibliographical references (p.).
    ISBN 0-937354-55-4 (pbk.)
    1. Refugees--Education--Asia, Southeastern.   2. Native language
and education--Asia, Southeastern.   3. Amerasians--Education.
4. Home and school--United States.   I. Ranard, Donald A. (Donald
Adam), 1945- .   II. Pfleger, Margo.   III. ERIC Clearinghouse on
Languages and Linguistics.   IV. Refugee Service Center.   V. Series.
LC3737.A785A76   1995
371.96'75'0959--dc20   95-7785
                                                                CIP

This book is dedicated to the 500,000 Vietnamese, Laotian, and Cambodian men, women, and children who studied in the overseas refugee program.

Language in Education: Theory and Practice

The Educational Resources Information Center (ERIC), which is supported by the Office of Educational Research and Improvement of the U.S. Department of Education, is a nationwide system of information centers, each responsible for a given educational level or field of study. ERIC's basic objective is to make developments in educational research, instruction, and teacher training readily accessible to educators and members of related professions.

The ERIC Clearinghouse on Languages and Linguistics (ERIC/CLL), one of the specialized information centers in the ERIC system, is operated by the Center for Applied Linguistics (CAL) and is specifically responsible for the collection and dissemination of information on research in languages and linguistics and on the application of research to language teaching and learning.

In 1989, CAL was awarded a contract to expand the activities of ERIC/CLL through the establishment of an adjunct ERIC clearinghouse, the National Clearinghouse for ESL Literacy Education (NCLE). NCLE's specific focus is literacy education for language minority adults and out-of-school youth.

ERIC/CLL and NCLE commission recognized authorities in languages, linguistics, adult literacy education, and English as a second language (ESL) to write about current issues in these fields. Monographs, intended for educators, researchers, and others interested in language education, are published under the series title, *Language in Education: Theory and Practice (LIE)*. The *LIE* series includes practical guides for classroom teachers, state-of-the-art papers, research reviews, and collected reports.

For further information on the ERIC system, ERIC/CLL, or NCLE, contact either clearinghouse at the Center for Applied Linguistics, 1118 22nd Street NW, Washington DC 20037.

Vickie W. Lewelling, ERIC/CLL Publications Coordinator
Miriam J. Burt, NCLE Publications Coordinator

Contents

Acknowledgments

Our special thanks belong to Douglas F. Gilzow, Language Training Specialist with the U.S. Peace Corps in Washington, DC, for his insightful suggestions, careful editing, faithful support, good humor, and firsthand knowledge of the overseas refugee training program.

We also want to express appreciation to the following people who helped review drafts of this volume. Many were personally involved in the overseas program, and all have been active in serving the needs of refugees and immigrants. Their valuable suggestions improved the accuracy, cohesiveness, and usefulness of this book.

Michele Burtoff Civan
Research Associate
Center for Applied Linguistics

John M. Duffy
Doctoral candidate
University of Wisconsin-Madison

Marilyn K. Gillespie
Senior Program Associate
Center for Applied Linguistics

Norma González
Assistant Research Anthropologist
University of Arizona

Allene Guss Grognet
Vice-President
Center for Applied Linguistics

David W. Haines
Author

Else V. Hamayan
Director of Training
Illinois Resource Center

Al Hoel
Instructional Program Director
The Consortium/World Learning
Bangkok, Thailand

Dora Johnson
Senior Program Associate
Center for Applied Linguistics

Fred Ligon
Deputy Instructional Program Director
The Consortium/World Learning
Phanat Nikhom, Thailand

Lynelle Long
US Agency for International Development

Nick Miscione
Project Director
International Catholic Migration Commission
Zagreb, Croatia

Shep Lowman
Director of International Refugee Affairs
Migration and Refugee Services
United States Catholic Conference

Eric Nadelstern
Principal
International High School
LaGuardia Community College

John E. Nelson
Parent Involvement Specialist
ESOL/Language Minority Program
Prince George's County (Maryland) Public
Schools

David S. North
New TransCentury Foundation

Joy Kreeft Peyton
Director, National Clearinghouse for
ESL Literacy Education
Center for Applied Linguistics

Klaudia Rivera
Director
El Barrio Popular

Mitzi Schroeder
Director of Washington DC Office
International Catholic Migration Commission

Heide Spruck Wrigley
Senior Research Associate
Aguirre International

G. Richard Tucker
Professor of Modern Languages
Carnegie Mellon University

Carol Toone
Educational Consultant
Woodson Adult Center
Fairfax County (Virginia) Public Schools

Maureen Webster
Executive Director
Catholic Social Service of Phoenix, Arizona

Photographs for this book were contributed by the following individuals: Charoensak Chongcharueyskul, Victoria C. Garcia, Roger E. Harmon, Passana Poo-roong, Donald A. Ranard, Elizabeth Tannenbaum, and Susan Willett. Other photographs were contributed by the International Catholic Migration Commission and the United Nations High Commissioner for Refugees.

Preface

This book is about a 15-year experiment in refugee education. From 1980 to 1995, the U.S. Department of State funded an intensive English language and cultural orientation program that prepared refugees living in camps in Southeast Asia for life in the United States. The success of this program led to the creation of smaller-scale efforts in other parts of the world, and today, pre-resettlement programs take place in Kenya and Croatia for U.S.-bound African and Bosnian refugees. This book focuses on the program in Southeast Asia because it was by far the largest of the overseas programs. Over the course of 15 years, about 500,000 Vietnamese, Laotian, and Cambodian refugees studied in camps in Hong Kong, Thailand, Indonesia, and the Philippines.

The overseas program represents a unique experiment in American history, and information about the program should be of interest to a wide range of readers. The book's primary audience, however, will be educators. The overseas program was a place where some of the newest ideas in language and cross-cultural education were proposed, debated, and tested. The principal purpose of this book is to document some of the program's best work and to share it with other refugee educators.

Those who want to learn more about the overseas program can find many of its reports, instructional materials, and student work in an archival collection housed at the Center for Applied Linguistics in Washington, DC and at World Learning in Brattleboro, Vermont.

Donald A. Ranard and Margo Pfleger, Editors

Chapter One
Balancing the Ideal and the Pragmatic

Ann Morgan

Balancing the Ideal and the Pragmatic

Reflections on the Overseas Refugee Program

Ann Morgan
U.S. Department of State

Since 1980, the Department of State has funded pre-entry training for refugees accepted for resettlement in the United States. The training programs have varied in size, location, focus, duration, and purposes; the student populations have also changed over time. The 15-year effort is unprecedented in the history of refugee migrations into the United States: For the first time, the U.S. government has provided refugees with skills needed for resettlement before they enter the United States.

Vietnamese boat people, hilltribe people from Laos, Amerasians from Vietnam, Cambodians fleeing from the Khmer Rouge, Ethiopians and Eastern Europeans escaping repressive regimes, Bosnians persecuted after Yugoslavia broke apart—these and others have participated in programs designed to meet their special needs. Nearly a million refugees have benefited; hundreds of organizations have played a role; dozens of governments have been involved.

Over the years, training programs were implemented in 15 countries where refugees sought protection while they applied for resettlement in the United States and other countries. By far the largest of these programs operated in Southeast Asia in refugee processing centers established in Indonesia, Thailand, and the Philippines. Because of their size and longevity, this book focuses on the programs in Thailand and the Philippines, which flourished for almost 15 years.

Responding to the Crisis

After the 1975 fall of the U.S.-supported governments in Vietnam, Laos, and Cambodia, it was inevitable that the United States would admit large numbers of refugees fleeing Southeast Asia. Closely associated with the United States, many could lay claim to a legitimate fear of persecution by new and repressive regimes. They would come and bring their relatives.

America saw and remembered the poignant pictures of terrified Vietnamese left behind when it closed its embassy in Saigon in 1975. Four years later, America saw and responded generously to media coverage of boat people fleeing Vietnam and of sick and starving Cambodians, victims of the genocidal Khmer Rouge, struggling into Thailand. The United States opened its doors wide.

Although public policy was generous in its response to the refugee crisis, there was concern that the entry of thousands of Southeast Asian refugees without English and basic orientation to American life might trigger a backlash. There was reason for concern. Almost overnight the refugee influx had altered the complexion of communities around the United States. Racial and ethnic balances were disturbed. Cultural clashes were commonplace. Disputes over fishing rights between Texas shrimpers and refugee fishermen from Vietnam were front-page news.

Stories of problems arising from cultural misunderstandings circulated in the resettlement community. Refugees were jailed for hunting without licenses—a restriction unheard of in their countries of origin. Parents were accused of child abuse when they left young children to supervise younger siblings—a common practice in many Asian countries. One refugee lost a hand to a garbage disposal he did not know how to use. Another died from drinking poison from a bottle labeled in English—a language she couldn't read. As these incidents grew in number, so did concern about how to prepare the refugees and to minimize public disapproval by providing refugees with basic information about life in the United States.

U.S.-bound refugees spent an average of six months at a processing center, such as this one in the Philippines.

The Need for Processing Centers

No serious thought was ever given to establishing large-scale training programs in the United States. Among a host of other problems, they were simply too expensive. A residential program in the United States comparable in content and duration to an overseas program would cost approximately five times as much.

The answer to the question of how to prepare thousands of Asian refugees for transition to America was to establish refugee processing and training centers in Southeast Asia. These centers had the capacity to address a number of problems. They provided a safe haven for refugees in danger of being pushed away from countries where they first landed after leaving their homes. They served as a safety valve for these countries of asylum, which had domestic problems with admitting—even temporarily—large numbers of refugees. Governments of countries providing temporary safe haven needed a place to send refugees when the population grew too large and they risked public opposition from their own citizens. Moreover, the United States and other countries of resettlement needed a place and time to process refugees in an orderly fashion. A facility was also needed where refugees could receive training while they waited for assurances of sponsorship from resettlement agencies in the United States. In response to these problems and needs, the processing centers in Southeast Asia came to be.

Thailand, the Philippines, Indonesia, and Malaysia allowed processing centers to be built within their borders. Thailand and Malaysia restricted access to refugees who crossed into those countries on their own; Indonesia and the Philippines allowed the international community to send refugees to their countries from other countries of first asylum. (See Chapter 2 for additional information on the Southeast Asia refugee crisis and the U.S. response.)

Securing Funding: Convincing Critics

Once the centers were in place, the next hurdle was to find a way to use them for training purposes. The vehicle chosen for funding was one of the many unusual aspects of this program. The agency charged with responsibility for implementation of training was the Department of State. Why? Such a task is not a common component of a foreign affairs portfolio. Why not the Department of Education or the Department of Health and Human Services? Both agencies funded and monitored training programs; the Department of State did not. The Department of State did, however, have long experience operating overseas and dealing with foreign governments. Any training undertaken in a foreign country would involve negotiations with other governments and would have to be tied closely to U.S. refugee admissions policy. For these reasons, the Refugee Act of 1980 gave the Department of State authority to undertake refugee training overseas and assigned responsibility for refugee training in the United States to the Department of Health and Human Services. With this authority granted by the Refugee Act, the Department of State could and did seek money for overseas training and, through the United Nations High Commissioner for Refugees, selected private, nongovernmental organizations to implement the programs in Southeast Asia.

Was it a good idea to provide training overseas? There are different views on this subject. One school of thought maintains that the "sink or swim" approach employed in earlier periods of heavy immigration into the United States should have been good enough. "My grandfather made out just fine without help from the government, so why shouldn't the same be true for refugees from Southeast Asia?" Advocates of this approach forget that many entrants into the United States between 1880 and 1920 were not refugees, but immigrants. They made a conscious choice to leave their countries—unlike refugees, who came because they had to. That is an important distinction when one thinks about preparation for change. The other contrast is that earlier waves of both refugees and immigrants entered a country where the skills they brought with them were easily transferrable, and daily life was not too different with respect to technology. Farmers and coal miners, blacksmiths and tailors could find comparable work in the America of yesterday. It was not so easy for the rice farmers or tricycle drivers from Cambodia and Laos to transfer their skills into productive employment in the America of today. Overseas training would give U.S.-bound refugees some orientation to a new life and minimize the anticipated backlash against them. Advocates of overseas training also made the case that it was cost-effective in the long run to ease new refugees' integration into American society and certainly more responsible in the short run to prepare them for the trauma of relocation.

With centers in place and with the authority and funds for training, the Department of State faced the challenge of how to do something that had never been done before. Although educators and other U.S. service providers had learned a great deal about how to help newly arrived refugees adjust to their new communities, no one had devised a training program for refugees before they entered the United States. There was widespread disagreement about the appropriate focus and content of training, with as many ideas about content as there were people involved in the refugee resettlement effort. There were two basic questions: What do refugees need to know before entering the United States?; and How much of it could be taught effectively in a transit situation in another country by non-American teachers?

The resulting debates were many. Perhaps the most important was the question of how much weight to assign to early employment. From the outset, refugee training both in the United States and overseas was justified by studies concluding that proficiency in English enhanced a refugee's employment potential and hastened self-sufficiency (Caplan, Whitmore, & Bui, 1985; Opportunity Systems, Inc., 1979; U.S. Department of Health and Human Services, 1982). While this may seem self-evident, there were those who argued that English proficiency was irrelevant because the United States made public assistance too attractive to pass up—particularly in welfare-generous states such as California and Minnesota. Why should refugees take entry-level jobs that usually paid no benefits when public assistance provided more money, and health coverage, as well? Refugees are not irrational people. They are likely to act in their own best interests, irrespective of the pesky, broader questions of how to keep America's gates open, provide newly arrived refugees with a safety net, and maintain public support in the face of growing opposition to a large influx of non-European newcomers.

In any event, it was clear that a justification for pre-entry training in the early 1980s required the argument that learning English made it easier to find and keep a job in America. Most of us who were engaged in pre-entry training accepted this argument. Although we knew that most refugees would take advantage of public assistance for some period of time, we also believed that in the long run, refugees would need less assistance if they knew English and had some knowledge of the new culture. This cannot be proven, and this book will make no effort to do so. What we can say is that if states with extremely attractive welfare benefits are exempted from the equation, most refugees used public assistance for a relatively short period of time and for its intended purpose. The crux of the matter was our conviction that English proficiency would help refugees become self-sufficient over time, thus improving their standard of living, and that language skills would ease their transition into a new culture. There has been no consistent government position respecting this issue. In the early 1980s, when money was available for language training, it was viewed as important. When funds became scarce, it wasn't. As in many other instances, the availability of resources strongly influenced public policy respecting language education.

Educational Goals

The role of English in achieving self-sufficiency, although of practical importance in securing funding for the program, was not the only area of interest to us in our role as educators. We saw our primary task as one of developing an appropriate course of instruction that addressed the needs of the refugee as a whole person.

Although English instruction occupied a central place in the curriculum, there were many other elements of equal importance. In cultural orientation classes, the goal was to balance information-giving with experiential involvement in understanding differences without judging. At the same time, we thought it was important for students to know that certain traditional practices could not be continued in the United States without censure and negative consequences. A particularly dramatic example is the Hmong custom of a young man abducting the 13- or 14-year-old girl he intends to marry.

We wanted students to understand the multiracial, multiethnic nature of American society. Since many refugee students came from relatively homogeneous societies, they had little experience with racial, ethnic, or religious differences. We wanted them to be prepared for the new experience of living and working in harmony with people very different from themselves.

We came to see retention of the native language as an important element of cultural identity and consequently made a place for

Educating refugee children is considered important because they represent the future of their families.

native language literacy in the program in Thailand. This aspect of the program is treated separately in Chapter 5 of this book, but is mentioned here as an example of the importance placed on retaining pride in one's native culture and heritage.

One constraint with which we wrestled was the initial imperative to focus on the adult within the refugee family who was most likely to be employed in the United States. There was not enough classroom space in the camps in the beginning to teach everyone in the family. As a result, one potential wage earner, usually a man, was selected from each household to participate.

Fortunately, from our perspective, this was a short phase. The student caseload soon became sufficiently manageable to include all adults over the age of sixteen. But, for us as educators, this was still not satisfactory. We saw refugee children and adolescents as equally important—if not more important—candidates for instruction, since they, after all, represented the future of their families and their communities. At the first opportunity, the student population was expanded to include refugees of high school age and, shortly thereafter, elementary school children in programs designed to mirror U.S. schools. In Thailand, preschoolers participated in programs patterned on Project Head Start.

To meet the widest range of needs, the training program developed learning centers, libraries, and other outside-the-classroom resources.

Over time, we were able to tailor the adult program to the particular needs of different groups. Young adults, whose futures in their new country were uncertain, participated in a program based on the exploration of choices. Mothers likely to be homebound attended special classes that recognized the reality of their resettlement experiences. Deaf students were taught sign language, and classes were established for refugees of all ages who had learning problems. Special needs were met not only in the classroom, but also in learning centers established to provide more individualized support.

In the final years of the program, we focused on intergenerational and family issues. We wanted students to anticipate how traditional roles might change and think ahead about ways of retaining their own cultural identity within the crucible of clashing values that is America. Refugees needed to be prepared for changes that would take place within the family as new economic pressures, new cultural influences, and different levels of English proficiency affected traditional roles within the family unit. Older children, for example, might acquire English faster than their parents, and would therefore play new and more assertive roles as intermediaries with landlords, physicians, service providers, and others. Women might be employed outside the home for the first time, thus changing dramatically their traditional roles.

Measuring Success

Were we successful in achieving all the objectives we set for ourselves? We think so. Some objectives are measurable. We know from the results of an intensive testing program that refugees made impressive strides in English proficiency during their course of study (Center for Applied Linguistics, 1988). We know from longitudinal studies done in the United States that secondary students who completed the program were viewed by their teachers as better prepared in all respects for the U.S. school experience than their refugee peers who did not participate (Pfleger & Yang, 1987). Based on this kind of objective measurement, we believe we can say with confidence that English instruction was a success.

But what about the other objectives considered important? How does one measure the acquisition of self-confidence? An increase in self-esteem? Attitudinal change? There might have been psychometric instruments that could have yielded quantifiable data about these elements of training, but we were unable to find practical measurement tools that could be applied in a program of such magnitude. After subjective observation, staff would say that results were positive in most cases, but it is not easy to measure intangibles. We can say only that we made a good-faith effort to provide information that would help refugees understand the new culture in which they would soon live and work.

In the final analysis, we must look to the refugees themselves for answers to the questions of whether the program worked or whether it was worth the extraordinary effort it required. In polling a sample of resettled refugees in America, almost 90% said that pre-entry training was useful and that they would recommend it to relatives who might join them in America—even if participation delayed their arrival in the country (RMC Research Corporation, 1984). Theirs are the most important of all voices. There are many who claim to speak for refugees, and many tools that can be employed to measure achievement, but only the refugees themselves can assess the value of the program in their own lives. This is the only yardstick that truly counts.

Intergenerational and family issues became an important program focus in the 1990s.

References

Caplan, N., Whitmore, J.K., & Bui, Q.L. (1985, January). *Southeast Asian refugee self-sufficiency study: Final report* (Contract No. HHS-100-81-0064). Prepared for Office of Refugee Resettlement, U.S. Department of Health and Human Services. Ann Arbor, MI: The Institute for Social Research.

Center for Applied Linguistics, Refugee Service Center. (1988, September). *Southeast Asia refugee testing report: Year 4.* Washington, DC: Author.

Opportunity Systems, Inc. (1979). *Eighth wave report: Indochinese resettlement operational feedback.* Washington, DC: Author.

Pfleger, M., & Yang, D. (1987, July). *The PASS tracking study: Final report to the Bureau for Refugee Programs, U.S. Department of State.* Washington, DC: Center for Applied Linguistics.

RMC Research Corporation. (1984, October). *The effects of pre-entry training on the resettlement of Indochinese refugees: Public report.* Hampton, NH: Author.

U.S. Department of Health and Human Services, Office of Refugee Resettlement. (1982, January 31). *Report to the Congress: Refugee resettlement program.* Washington, DC: U.S. Government Printing Office.

Post Script: Lessons for Management

One of the unique aspects of the program was the nature of the partnership it created between government and private agencies. At its height, overseas training spanned four continents, operated in 15 sites, and involved 11 nongovernmental organizations. More than 2,000 nationals of host countries were employed by the implementing agencies as teachers, supervisors, and support staff.

From the beginning, the agencies implementing the program were an integral part of the planning, policymaking, and curriculum development. Over the years, the relationship between the Department of State and its implementing partners in refugee education became increasingly symbiotic, each element depending for its success on the cooperation and support of the other. The lessons learned during the evolution of this partnership are not revolutionary in the field of management, but they may be instructive and relevant to any endeavor requiring a productive relationship between government and private organizations. These lessons are discussed here in the context of delivering educational services overseas, but the principles involved are applicable to any partnership between the public and private sectors.

1. Work Cooperatively to Establish Objectives.

As the funding source, the Department of State established a program framework at the onset to estimate and contain costs. That framework was skeletal but defining. It set forth the broad goals of providing English and cultural orientation to U.S.-bound refugees within a given number of weeks, required that teachers be nationals of the host country, and stipulated that all teachers receive 10 hours of teacher training per week. It included guidelines respecting ratios of students to teachers and of teachers to supervisors. It required testing and evaluation and promoted common content within different programs in a region. All programs, irrespective of site, were required to follow these guidelines.

For curriculum content, the Department of State looked to a wide range of people. Refugees, program managers, resettlement workers, educators, psychologists, social workers, government officials— all had roles to play in deciding the content and objectives of the programs. Their expertise was needed repeatedly as the nature of the refugee student population changed. For example, special attention was given to hilltribe students, young adult refugees, pregnant women and women with young children, and children headed for U.S. elementary and secondary schools.

Involvement took many forms, and many different approaches to reaching consensus were employed. Workshops attended by educators and other service providers were held both in the United States and in Southeast Asia. Regional meetings involving staff from all overseas training sites were held on a regular basis. Sites frequently exchanged staff: Supervisors and teachers from the Philippines went to Thailand and vice versa. Program-produced newsletters and journals shared ideas and information among overseas staff and service providers in the United States. Resettlement workers, including resettled refugees, were invited to visit the overseas programs. At the same time, meetings among heads of implementing agencies and government officials in the United States continued to shape program direction.

2. Let Managers Manage.

This precept is axiomatic in business. Implicit in this statement is the expectation that staff hired to perform tasks that cannot be done by the funding source are competent and should be permitted to function without undue interference. In supporting overseas training, the Department of State was operating outside its traditional mandate. Faced with the task of developing instructional guidelines or addressing curriculum issues such as adult literacy or competency-based instruction, the Department of State had to look outside itself for expertise and rely heavily on the collective judgment of implementing agencies. This encouraged active cooperation and collaboration.

While the guidelines established by the Department of State were respected, as were collective decisions about content, each agency was given a great deal of freedom in choice of methodology. This led to much experimentation, encouraged creativity and innovation, and resulted in healthy competition among agencies. Duplication of effort was avoided by institutionalized information sharing and exchanges of staff in the field.

This is not to say that management was always smooth or that the implementation of a program of this magnitude was without its problems. It was not. Not everyone, for example, agreed with the notion of regional standards or testing. Nor was everyone comfortable, especially in the beginning, with such close cooperation with other agencies usually seen as competitors. Over time, however, institutional competition diminished as people came to trust one another and to appreciate the value of pooling their strengths.

Most important, program directors in the field had authority to manage their operations as they saw fit within the guidelines agreed upon. The Department of State and the home offices of the implementing agencies made every effort to avoid micromanagement.

3. Expect to Pay to Be the Best.

Funding entities must be willing to pay for what they demand. This often means picking up the tab for some portion of the costs for home office operations of private agencies. It also means that government must be prepared to pay a competitive rate for the services of competent individuals. Nonprofit organizations employ professionals who deserve compensation for what they do. The erroneous notion has crept into the minds of some government managers that nongovernmental staff are somehow entitled to less than one would pay others whose world view does not value service to others. It is the same mind set that keeps the compensation of teachers in many of our public schools at low levels and results in the exploitation of dedicated people in many service occupations.

It is also important not to underestimate the importance of staff training. One often hears organizations say they can afford neither the time nor the money for staff training. On the contrary, an organization that expects to realize its full potential cannot afford *not* to provide staff training in a regular and organized fashion.

4. Build a Partnership.

The "enabling instruments," which define the relationship between government and private cooperating partners, should be as simple and flexible as possible. There are many different types of enabling instruments. They all codify the rules governing resources and ensure that proper accounting takes place. The one most commonly used by government is the contract, in which the funding entity spells out in detail what it wants and expects. A less common—but, in my view, more effective—enabling instrument is the cooperative agreement. Unlike the contract, the cooperative agreement incorporates the principles of partnership between the funding entity and the implementing organization. At the same time, it clearly defines the roles of each partner. It allows for flexibility and can easily be amended if tasks are revised or responsibilities change.

The cooperative agreement also permits the funding entity to request reports tailored to the needs of the program. While it is important to monitor carefully the expenditure of funds and to ensure that reports provide enough information to do so, paperwork can be reduced to a minimum.

5. Make Evaluation a Priority.

Whatever vehicle is used to establish the rules, there must be clear and objective standards against which success can be measured, and partners should have a role in developing those standards. In the overseas program, partners outlined goals and objectives in an annual management plan. These plans, written by the private agencies with overall direction from the Department of State, were used to monitor progress.

6. Build In the Capacity for Change.

In any good social service program, there must be a capacity to change quickly. In the overseas program, change was one of the few constants. Each new refugee population brought new challenges requiring adjustments in approach or curriculum. To make these adjustments it was often necessary to bring in consultants or to convene large meetings quickly. It is extremely difficult to do this within government, so it is essential to have an umbrella organization that is not involved directly in managing a training program but that can function as an extension of the funding source. Responding to public inquiries, developing specialized materials, providing technical assistance, supervising testing and evaluation, distributing materials, convening special meetings and events—all these functions are important but are difficult to manage within a bureaucracy that is not established to handle them.

Chapter Two
Responding to the Crisis

Roger E. Harmon

Roger E. Harmon

Responding to the Crisis

Creation of the Overseas Refugee Program

Roger E. Harmon
International Organization for Migration
Bangkok, Thailand

Many believe that the flight [of refugees from Vietnam, Laos and Cambodia] has only begun, and that at least 1 million (and perhaps 2–3 million) more people may be fleeing from their homes in the coming months and years. The world is unprepared in every way for this eventuality.

Indochina Refugee Action Center, *Issue Paper: Synopsis of Current Indochinese Refugee Situation,* 1979

Though the world was unprepared for the Southeast Asia refugee challenge, an intensive effort was initiated in 1979 to meet it. This chapter discusses a part of that effort, the creation of intensive overseas training for refugees resettling in the United States, focusing particularly on events and conditions in Southeast Asia and in the United States that led to the startup of the program.

From 1950 to 1980, refugees bound for the United States received little or no cultural orientation or language training prior to their departure. Rather, orientation and language training were offered in the United States by the sponsors, agencies, and schools in the community of resettlement. An exception to this pattern of local services was the training offered to Hungarians in the 1950s and to first-wave Indochinese in 1975. Upon arrival in the United States, these two groups were housed briefly in U.S. military bases, where they were offered optional cultural orientation and English language classes until sponsorship in an American community could be arranged. Other groups arriving during the period 1976 to 1979—Cubans, Haitians, Soviet Jews, and the Indochinese—went directly to U.S. communities without benefit of training.

Why, then, in the absence of any precedent, was an overseas training program for Southeast Asian refugees established in 1980? To answer this question, we need to look at the realities in Southeast Asia and the United States at that time.

Realities in Southeast Asia and the United States

The first groups of Indochinese refugees fled their countries in the spring of 1975, shortly after the fall of U.S.-supported governments in Vietnam, Laos, and Cambodia. These first-wave refugees were mostly Vietnamese and included many members of the former government. Nearly 130,000 resettled in the United States.

In the late 1970s, war, persecution, and poverty in Indochina unleashed a second exodus, by land and sea, of hundreds of thousands of people. Refugee camps sprung up across Southeast Asia to provide safe haven to the fleeing families. By mid-1979, while more than 400,000 Indochinese had been resettled in Western countries, nearly 400,000 remained in refugee camps. Thailand bore the greatest brunt of the influx. As of July 1979, the refugee camp population in first-asylum countries was as follows (Indochina Refugee Action Center, 1979, p. 4):

Thailand	176,651
Hong Kong/Macau	69,917
Malaysia	61,559
Indonesia	55,000 (est.)
Philippines	5,794
Other	2,650

This second wave of refugees was different in several ways from the first. The most dramatic difference between the two was size, but there were other differences as well. In contrast to the first, the second wave included large numbers of refugees from Laos and

Before arriving in the processing centers, many refugee families spent months—and sometimes years— in first-asylum camps.

Cambodia. The second wave also included ethnic minorities. Many of the boat people fleeing Vietnam were in fact ethnic Chinese, and the flow of refugees from Cambodia included Chinese, Vietnamese, and Chams, a Muslim minority. The ethnic diversity of the refugee population from Laos was greatest. In addition to the majority Lao, the refugee population from that country included the Hmong, Mien, and Thai Dam, each with a distinctive language and culture.

Another difference between the two groups was in levels of education and familiarity with urban life. The second wave included many more refugees from rural areas who had, on the whole, less formal education and less previous contact with Westerners and modern technology (Caplan, Whitmore, & Choy, 1989; Rumbaut, 1985; U.S. Department of Health and Human Services, 1983). This was particularly the case with the Hmong and the Mien, the great majority of whom were nonliterate.

The two groups also differed in the amount of hardship they had suffered. Unlike those who had fled Indochina on U.S. planes and ships in 1975, second-wave refugees experienced the hardship of life under the new regimes (some as political prisoners) and suffered harrowing escapes by sea and land. No group suffered more than the Cambodian refugees, survivors of civil war, genocide, famine, and brutal conditions in the Thai-Cambodian border camps (Hamilton, 1982).

The continuing flow of large numbers of refugees led Southeast Asian first-asylum countries to reassess their willingness to help, and to call for greater support from the rest of the world. In 1979, international organizations and concerned governments stepped up efforts to alleviate the situation. The immediate challenge was to ensure the survival of refugees fleeing by sea and by land. The media reported countless stories of boats of Vietnamese refugees being pushed away as they attempted to land on the shores of neighboring countries. As early as 1979, estimates of the number of Vietnamese lost at sea ranged from thousands to hundreds of thousands (Indochina Refugee Action Center, 1979). Some refugees fleeing overland into Thailand—mostly from Laos and Cambodia, but a small number from Vietnam, as well—were pushed back at the Thai border.

Viewing Indochinese refugees as a potential threat to the region's economic and political stability, Southeast Asian countries would not allow asylum seekers to settle permanently. Loescher and Scanlan (1986) explain Thai and Malaysian attitudes toward the refugee influx.

Thai authorities, particularly the military, saw the refugee influx as giving immense potential for disruption and as an increased security threat. . . . Malaysia was concerned that the flow of Vietnamese boat people, who were primarily ethnic Chinese, could upset the delicate domestic racial and political balance, particularly since they landed on the east coast of Malaysia, where the population was overwhelmingly rural Malay, devotedly Islamic, and poor. The refugees were pictured as a subtle invasion force from Vietnam and as a potential fifth column for a renewed Communist insurgency. (p. 125)

While Southeast Asian countries would not provide permanent asylum to refugees, they were willing to provide temporary safe haven in refugee camps funded and administered by the United Nations High Commissioner for Refugees (UNHCR). By 1980,

Compared to the refugees who fled their homelands in Southeast Asia in 1975, later groups tended to be more rural and less educated.

there were more than twenty of these first-asylum camps in Thailand, Malaysia, Indonesia, the Philippines, and Hong Kong (U.S. Department of State, 1981). Conditions in these camps were generally primitive, in part because there was concern that to provide more than basic services was to risk attracting more refugees. Humanitarian organizations attemping to improve the quality of camp life by offering refugees more than basic services often met with resistance from the UNHCR and host-country governments, which were sensitive to any action that might increase the flow of refugees. For this reason, educational services in first-asylum camps were limited, though modest efforts to teach English did exist, organized either by refugee relief agencies or by the refugees themselves.

As a quid pro quo for providing asylum to the large numbers of refugees continuing to flow out of Indochina, Southeast Asian countries wanted to see overall refugee numbers in their countries decline—or at least not dramatically increase. Since refugees could not remain in first-asylum countries nor safely return to their own, resettlement in third countries became the primary solution for Indochinese refugees through the 1970s and 1980s.

The United States' response to the international crisis was a commitment to resettle large numbers of these refugees. The Carter administration pledged to double the number of Indochinese refugees the United States would accept, from 7,000 per month to 14,000 (Loescher & Scanlan, 1986). Between 1979 and 1980, over 240,000 refugees were admitted to the United States directly from first-asylum camps.

In resettling larger numbers of Indochinese, the United States achieved its objectives of maintaining first asylum in Southeast Asia and honoring its commitment to its former allies in Vietnam, Laos, and Cambodia. The sheer size of the flow, however, threatened to exceed U.S. resettlement capacity. Overseas, the processing of refugees required a herculean effort in registering asylum seekers, determining who was eligible for refugee status and processsing applications for resettlement. In the United States, there were growing concerns about finding sponsors and about the capacity of communities to absorb large numbers of refugees in such a short period of time.

The solution to this dilemma was the creation of what became known as processing centers: transit camps for refugees from first-asylum camps who had been accepted for admission to the United States and other countries of resettlement. Created in 1980, these centers served two major purposes: They kept the population of first-asylum camps at lower levels, and they allowed for the possibility of an orderly, manageable flow of refugees into the United States. Three centers were established: one on the Bataan peninsula in the Philippines, one on the island of Galang in Indonesia, and one near Phanat Nikhom, Thailand, a small town southeast of Bangkok.

For the first time since the displaced persons camps after World War II, large numbers of refugees would be spending extended periods of time—more than a year, in some cases—in transit camps: "a strange netherworld of national/international jurisdiction" requiring "some special kind of management" (D. Haines, personal communication, December 1994). Populated largely with refugees bound for the United States, processing centers offered an ideal opportunity for a pre-resettlement education program.

Refugees over the age of 16 attended classes in English as a second language and cultural orientation.

Certainly there was mounting evidence that recently arrived refugees could use some kind of preparation. Having shifted at jet speed from first-asylum refugee camps to cities and suburbs across the United States, many second-wave refugees found themselves in linguistic and cross-cultural confusion. Many refugees, particularly those from the rural areas of Southeast Asia, were for the first time confronting life in a technological, urban society; many had never applied for a job before, operated modern appliances, or used Western medicine. Some could not read warning and danger signs and had no idea what to do in case of a household emergency. There were reports of widespread and serious mental health problems, particularly depression among refugees (Cohon, 1980; United Community Planning Corporation, 1982; Westermeyer, 1985). In one widely reported incident, a Hmong man, unable to understand what was happening to him and fearing that he had failed his wife and children, organized the mass suicide of his family (Trillin, 1980).

With little English or knowledge of the U.S. workplace, refugees had scant hope of finding jobs quickly. While many refugees went to work within the first few weeks of arriving in the United States, an increasing number turned to public assistance while they studied English in special programs. Refugees were eligible for cash and medical assistance during their first months in United States, but such assistance was intended to be used as a last resort. By 1979, concern was growing over the perceived trend of refugees being referred to local welfare agencies for public assistance as part of their *initial* settling-in process. Policymakers and service providers questioned whether it was possible to sustain support for continuing Indochinese refugee admissions if entering refugees chose welfare over work. A Department of State report noted that while refugees unquestionably needed some support,

It is equally important that [refugees] be, and be seen as, actively involved in developing their future. It is unhelpful if they are seen as receiving special benefits, not accorded others in the society, unless this can be clearly associated with temporary refugee needs leading to early integration and self-sufficiency for most. (U.S. Department of State, 1979, p. 12)

In some parts of the United States, the perception that large numbers of refugees were receiving special benefits contributed to tensions between new arrivals and local residents. As refugees competed with local residents for social services, low-income housing, jobs, and diminishing resources, resentment was voiced. Occasionally, this resentment resulted in violence.

These community conflicts and other problems aroused growing concern about the effectiveness of the resettlement system (Indochina Refugee Action Center, 1980a). A patchwork of providers, both public and private, attempted to meet the resettlement needs of the newcomers. Serving as the primary sponsor of each refugee and funded by the federal government, national voluntary agencies, known as "volags," were responsible for refugees' basic needs during their initial months in the United States. During the first few years of the Indochinese resettlement program, volags had used churches and synagogues, community organizations, and American families as secondary sponsors to take care of newly arrived refugees' day-to-day needs. The effort had been characterized by an extraordinary degree of volunteerism, but by the late 1970s the volume began to overwhelm the ability of the system to respond. Not enough sponsors were available, and volags turned to other sponsorship models.

By 1979, three additional methods of sponsorship were being utilized more frequently. One was the anchor relative model, in which a previously resettled relative assumed resettlement responsibilities. Another was the Indochinese group sponsorship, in which an Indochinese temple, church, or refugee self-help group provided initial services. Most common was the direct placement or casework model, in which local volag staff took over resettlement responsibilities (Indochina Refugee Action Center, 1980b). While this model had the potential to provide professional services to refugees, caseworkers found it difficult to meet the many needs of their large caseloads. The casework model was being used at a time when the network of supporters in the community needed to be broadened, not narrowed to a handful of professionals. Instead of being sponsored into an extended network of a church, synagogue, civic group, or family, more and more refugees were linked to their new communities through an agency caseworker, a recently resettled relative, or other members of their ethnic group—people whose ties to the community were often limited. The casework model did little to encourage the refugee to build a network of connections and support outside their own ethnic community.

In addition to the volag services, refugees received a wide array of federally funded social, medical, and educational services, yet increasingly there was concern that the range of services was inadequate to meet the pressing needs of the newcomers. State and local governments felt they should not be required to expend their resources on a "problem" rooted in federal policy and programs, and by the end of 1979, the federal government was being called upon to shoulder more of the burden.

Questions were raised about the U.S. capability to provide effective resettlement. Even the Indochinese resettled in 1975, considered by some to be a model group, were not adjusting so well, some observers noted. Hung (1985) cites a core difficulty. "Behind an appearance of economic success, Vietnamese refugees, especially the older ones, have not done equally well in social and psychological adjustment. Most have not made a conscious effort to integrate themselves into American society" (p. 203).

Federal, state, and local government officials, social service providers, voluntary agency officials, refugee self-help groups, and citizens joined the clamor over refugee issues. Initiatives funded by the federal government at the end of 1979 and early 1980 centered on collecting basic data on the resettlement situation and on soliciting views on how to strengthen resettlement. The newly created Office of the U.S. Coordinator for Refugee Affairs at the U.S. Department of State set up a series of work groups composed of representatives of governmental and nongovernmental organizations concerned with refugee resettlement. These efforts yielded recommendations that for the most part supported the basic resettlement system but called for additional federally funded services. Part of the call was for better preparation of refugees before they arrived in U.S. communities.

Overseas Refugee Training: Part of the Solution

Several proposals for orientation and language training in Southeast Asian camps were made by governmental and nongovernmental agencies between November 1979 and April 1980. Two Ford Foundation studies found little or no language and cultural orientation training in the Thai camps—a situation that existed in camps in other countries as well (Spaulding et al., 1979; Webb, Barnes, Buranasiri, & Griffin, 1980). The studies recommended strengthening existing efforts by providing materials and teacher training to the camps through a refugee service center in Bangkok. One of the proposals called for a 12-week program that would give the student command of at least "enough simple phrases to enter a third country and not be at a total linguistic loss" (Spaulding et al., 1979, p. 23).

Support for the notion of overseas training also came from the Work Group on Orientation, a task force set up by the Office of the U.S. Coordinator for Refugee Affairs. Concerned about the amount of time refugees might spend in the processing centers, the work group echoed the need expressed in the Ford Foundation studies for English language training and orientation "to ensure that the time spent waiting in such camps is used productively." The report suggested a two- to four-month survival English and orientation program.

The work group further recommended that specifications for an overseas program be drafted by March 1980, and the Indochina Refugee Action Center (IRAC) was designated to convene a task force to produce such a plan. IRAC—which later changed its name to Southeast Asia Resource Action Center (SEARAC)—is an umbrella organization for refugee self-help groups. The IRAC task force was made up of representatives from agencies conducting small-scale language and orientation programs in the camps as well as representatives from national and local resettlement agencies. Indochinese leaders also took part in the discussions.

Guided by the Department of State, the most likely funder of an overseas program, the IRAC task force developed specifications for a three-month training program to be offered immediately prior to the refugee's departure for the United States. The proposed program was for 15 to 20 hours of English as a second language (ESL) study and 6 to 8 hours of cultural orientation instruction per week, plus self-study. For ESL, priority would be given to all "potential wage-earners, including both men and women," age 16 and above. The IRAC task force suggested that, optimally, everyone over the age of 10 would receive cultural orientation. The task force made recommendations for both ESL and orientation programs regarding goals, content, methodology, materials, evaluation, and staff. The task force voiced concerns about the special needs of refugees with low levels of English proficiency, recommending native language literacy instruction for nonliterate students. The task force also recommended that the program take into account the needs of women and other special-needs groups. In addition, it proposed a regional service center in Southeast Asia to provide support to the camp programs and linkage with service providers in the United States (Indochina Refugee Action Center, 1980c).

The Refugee Act of 1980 had designated the Department of State as the lead U.S. government agency responsible for overseas refugee affairs, including training. The Department of State had been a principal participant in the IRAC meetings, and it acted quickly. In June 1980, the State Department funded UNHCR to establish intensive ESL and cultural orientation classes in refugee camps and processing centers in Thailand, Indonesia, the Philippines, and Hong Kong, and by that fall, the programs were operational. The programs in Thailand were operated by Pragmatics, Inc. and the Consortium, made up of the Experiment in International Living (now renamed World Learning), Save the Children, and World Education. The Experiment in International Living and Save the

Children jointly operated the program in Indonesia, while Lutheran Immigration and Refugee Service and American Council for Nationalities Service (now renamed Immigration and Refugee Services of America) operated the Hong Kong program. International Catholic Migration Commission managed the program in the Philippines, and the Center for Applied Linguistics provided support to the program sites through an office in Bangkok, later moved to Manila. In 1986, World Relief Corporation began operating a school for refugee children in the Philippine program. In the mid-1980s, as the number of refugees decreased, the overseas program consolidated training into two sites: Phanat Nikhom, Thailand, and the Philippine Refugee Processing Center. This book focuses on the educational programs at these two sites.

In its educational objectives, the overseas program began somewhat modestly, focusing on the basic English and cultural orientation refugees needed during their first few months in the United States. But over the years, the program grew in scope and sophistication, as we shall see in the following chapters.

References

References marked with an asterisk (*) are unpublished typescripts of limited circulation archived in a 3-volume collection, entitled Background on the Origin of the Overseas Refugee Training Program, *at the Center for Applied Linguistics, 1118 22nd Street NW, Washington DC 20037. The alphanumeric code in brackets denotes the document number in this collection.*

Caplan, N., Whitmore, J.K., & Choy, M.H. (1989). *The boat people and achievement in America: A study of family life, hard work, and cultural values.* Ann Arbor, MI: The University of Michigan Press.

Cohon, J.D. (1980, March). *Can TESOL teachers address the mental health concerns of the Indochinese refugees?* Paper presented at the 14th annual convention of TESOL, San Francisco, CA.

Hamilton, J.P. (1982). *Cambodian refugees in Thailand: The limits of asylum.* New York: American Council for Nationalities Service, U.S. Committee for Refugees.

Hung, N.M. (1985). Vietnamese. In D.W. Haines (Ed.), *Refugees in the United States: A reference handbook* (pp. 195-208). Westport, CT: Greenwood.

*Indochina Refugee Action Center. (1979, August 13). *Issue paper: Synopsis of current Indochinese refugee situation.* [A5]

*Indochina Refugee Action Center. (1980a, January 22). [Domestic Resettlement Planning Project (Airlie report)]. [A9]

*Indochina Refugee Action Center. (1980b, January). *Proposal: Orientation Resource Center.* [C5]

*Indochina Refugee Action Center (1980c, April 9). *Specifications for an intensive English as a second language and orientation program for Indochinese refugees in Southeast Asia.* [C8]

Loescher, G., & Scanlan, J.A. (1986). *Calculated kindness: Refugees and America's half-open door, 1945 to the present.* London: The Free Press.

Rumbaut, R.G. (1985). Mental health and the refugee experience: A comparative study of Southeast Asian refugees. In T.C. Owan (Ed.), *Southeast Asian mental health: Treatment, prevention, services, training, and research* (pp. 433-486). Washington, DC: National Institute of Mental Health.

*Spaulding, S., Ford, D., Grognet, A., Lehman, J., Prasertsri, S., Saengchantr, C., & Wongchalard, W. (1979, December 3). *A refugee education resource center in Thailand with a recommended language and orientation program for refugee camps and transit centers. A needs assessment and preliminary proposal prepared by a World Education, Inc., study team, for the Ford Foundation.* [C3]

Trillin, C. (1980, March 24). U.S. journal: Fairfield, Iowa. *The New Yorker*, pp. 83-100.

United Community Planning Corporation. (1982). *Needs assessment of Southeast Asian refugee population in Massachusetts.* Boston, MA: Author.

U.S. Department of Health and Human Services, Office of Refugee Resettlement. (1983, January 31). *Report to the Congress: Refugee resettlement program.* Washington, DC: Author.

U.S. Department of State, Bureau for Refugee Programs. (1981). *Summary of refugee admissions for fiscal year 1981.* Washington, DC: Author.

*U.S. Department of State, Refugee Program/Office of Asian Refugees. (n.d., ca. 1979). [Resettlement problems and recommendations]. [A4]

*Webb, J., Barnes, R., Buranasiri, S., & Griffin, B. (1980, January). *Refugee orientation: Part I. A proposal for immediate action.* [C4]

Westermeyer, J. (1985). Mental health of Southeast Asian refugees: Observations over two decades from Laos and the United States. In T.C. Owan (Ed.), *Southeast Asian mental health: Treatment, prevention, services, training, and research* (pp. 65-89). Washington, DC: National Institute of Mental Health.

Chapter Three
Redefining Survival

**Donald A. Ranard
& Margo Pfleger**

Redefining Survival

Practices, Trends, and Issues in the Overseas Refugee Program

Donald A. Ranard and Margo Pfleger
Center for Applied Linguistics

Launched in 1980 in response to the Southeast Asian refugee crisis, the overseas program began with a limited objective: to provide adult refugees from Vietnam, Laos, and Cambodia with the basic language skills and knowledge of American life they needed during their first few months in the United States. At refugee camps and processing centers in Hong Kong, Indonesia, Thailand, and the Philippines, the program operated in makeshift schoolhouses with little more than chalkboards and chairs. Chinese, Indonesian, Thai, and Filipino teachers taught ESL and cultural orientation classes emphasizing language-related lifeskills and information about resettlement. Refugees studied 4 hours a day for 12 weeks, in morning or afternoon sessions, attending to children and chores during the other half of the day. Few learning opportunities existed outside the classrooms.

By late 1994, as the last groups of refugees studied in the overseas program, almost every aspect of the program had changed. The program's six sites had been consolidated into two—the Philippine Refugee Processing Center and Phanat Nikhom Refugee Camp in Thailand. From primitive camps that met only the most basic needs, both had evolved into full-fledged communities that included open-air markets, temples and churches, hospitals, mental health clinics, childcare facilities, soccer fields, restaurants, and outdoor cafes. The educational facilities had expanded, integrating the once-simple classrooms into a community of learning, complete with libraries, listening labs, multimedia learning centers, and recreational facilities. Instruction also had kept pace with changes in the dynamic field of refugee education: By 1994, a program that had focused on survival English and cultural orientation for adult heads of household was providing family members of all ages, from tots to seniors, a full range of educational and social services, both inside and outside the classroom.

Educating Adult Refugees

Initially, the program limited services to adult refugees, 16 to 55 years of age: those considered most responsible for their families' economic futures. During a half-day of instruction, refugees studied English and learned about American life in cultural orientation classes taught in the native language.

ESL students were placed into one of five proficiency levels, A through E, with the A level for students not literate in any language. Class size was limited to 20, with A-level classes often smaller. Cultural orientation classes, grouped by learners' language backgrounds, were generally larger. A small number of English-proficient refugees placed out of the ESL instruction. These refugees served as classroom aides or performed other educational roles.

In 1983, two years after the program had begun, a third component, work orientation, was added, extending training to 20 weeks. Taught in English, work orientation classes grouped students by ESL proficiency.

In designing the initial program, staff built upon small-scale English language and cultural orientation efforts already underway in the camps and incorporated new developments from the emerging field of refugee education.

English as a Second Language

In designing the ESL curriculum, staff drew on the competency-based movement that was gaining popularity among U.S. refugee educators in the late 1970s. Teaching English within the context of lifeskills, competency-based ESL marked a departure from the grammar-based approach that had dominated the field in the 1960s and early 1970s. Teaching language in the

Donald A. Ranard & Margo Pfleger

Large-scale simulations enabled students to apply what they had learned in ESL and cultural orientation classes. Here, beginning-level students purchase tickets at a simulated cinema.

context of real-life tasks—requesting medical help, reading want ads, filling out forms—competency-based language instruction connected the classroom to the community. For overseas staff, the approach had immediate appeal: It was practical, it gave teachers and students a clear sense of purpose and direction, and it put into practice some of the latest theories about effective, learner-centered language education.

Two early decisions strongly influenced the ESL curriculum development process in the overseas program. First, curriculum content would be limited to those competencies that refugees would need during their first few months in the United States (Corey, 1986). The second decision was to focus on listening and speaking, limiting reading and writing instruction to a small number of specific literacy tasks, such as reading important sight words, filling out a simple job application form, and finding a name and number in a telephone directory. The decision to limit literacy instruction was based in part on the belief that in the first months of resettlement, it was more important for refugees to understand and speak English than to read and write it. The decision also reflected the notion, held over from audiolingualism, that students needed to gain oral proficiency in a language before learning to read and write it.

The curriculum indicated course content but not how the content would be taught. Turning competencies into lively, effective language lessons absorbed the energy and imagination of staff over the next few years. Two principles of language learning emerged: Learners learn best when they are actively engaged and when they use language for real-life purposes. Using realia to provide context, students conducted mock interviews with employers and reported emergencies over the telephone. Working in small groups, they planned household budgets and debated the pros and cons of public assistance. In large-scale clinic simulations, they filled out a medical history form, described their ailments to a nurse, listened to a doctor's treatment plan, and showed that they understood directions on a medicine bottle (Wheeler, 1986). A basic principle of instruction was to introduce the unknown by way of the known (Hiponia & Walker, 1983). A lesson on housing, for example, moved from a discussion of housing in the native country, to housing in the camp, to housing in the United States. This approach encouraged students to bring personal and community issues into the classroom, and through problem-posing, teachers integrated community concerns into their teaching (Wallerstein, 1983).

This kind of process-oriented, experiential approach was often at odds with the demands of the curriculum, however, as teachers discovered that there was simply not enough time to teach the way they were being trained to teach and cover all the material in the curriculum, too. There was also concern that the number of competencies did not allow enough time for overall language development (Kharde & Corey, 1986). Staff feared that without more attention to language development, competency-based instruction could become a phrase-book approach to language learning (Ranard & Pfleger, 1994). These concerns led ESL staff, working together with U.S. educators, to sort through the competencies, dropping those that were not critical or were better taught by U.S. programs. By 1984, these efforts had reduced the number of competencies by one third.

ESL Topics and Competencies in the Overseas Program

The overseas program's ESL competency-based curriculum organized language-related lifeskills by topic areas. Over the history of the program, the topics and competencies were changed in response to new refugee populations, new information about refugee resettlement, and new instructional approaches. As an example of this type of curriculum framework, the following is an edited list of intermediate-level competencies from the 1985 curriculum:

HEALTH

- Ask doctor/nurse about own physical condition or treatment plan using simple language.
- Describe symptoms associated with common illness.
- Read an appointment card, including time, date, and name of doctor/ nurse.
- Read signs for X-RAY, LAB, PHARMACY, and DRUGSTORE.
- Read and follow directions on medicine labels, including instructions and abbreviations. Read names of common nonprescription medicines.

HOUSING

- Ask for information about housing, including rent, deposit, location, and utilities.
- Arrange a time with landlord/superintendent to make household repairs.

EMPLOYMENT: FINDING A JOB

- Inquire about job openings and arrange for an interview in person.
- Ask and answer basic questions about pay, work availability, hours, work shifts, starting date, payday, and medical benefits.
- Answer basic questions about educational background, including dates and locations.
- Describe previous work experience, job skills, qualifications, and training, including some degree of ability.

With fewer competencies to cover, teachers paid more attention to learners' general language development, in particular to their literacy skills. While ESL educators once believed that students needed to develop oral proficiency before learning to read and write, now ESL educators argued that students could and should learn to read and write the new language at the same time they were learning to speak it; the four skills of listening, speaking, reading, and writing interacted in a supportive way, reinforcing one another, educators believed (Larsen-Freeman, 1986). Moreover, there was growing appreciation for literacy as an important source of information and as a tool for lifelong learning.

Among refugee educators overseas and in the United States, ESL literacy instruction became an area of lively debate and discussion, as programs dealt for the first time with large numbers of nonliterate learners. Overseas staff began experimenting with approaches to teaching literacy that tied instruction to students' lives. Coming from war-torn homelands, surviving dangerous escapes, and having spent months or years in isolated refugee camps, refugees brought to the classroom a rich variety of experiences, and increasingly teachers used these experiences as a basis for instruction. One staff member collected her students' stories into a book, *The New Arrival*, that became a popular reading text both in the overseas program and in U.S. programs (Kuntz, 1982). The refugee experience in America also enriched classroom instruction when staff collected letters from resettled refugees into texts (Riddle, 1985; Turner, Ligon, DiGregorio, LaMare, & Hicks, 1989). At one site, a shortage of beginning-level, high-interest commercial reading material led teachers and students to write, illustrate, and publish more than 50 short books, drawing on native folktales, refugee experiences, and aspects of American life that interested students (Aguilar, Blackstock, Mauricio, Snyder, & Walsh, 1988). In multimedia resource centers, students honed their emerging literacy skills as they read along with taped stories, wrote about films they had viewed, and composed conclusions to open-ended stories posted on bulletin boards on the walls.

Reading and writing also received more attention in upper-level ESL classes. A collection of authentic texts—maps, health history forms, car insurance information, lease agreements—provided students with the kinds of reading material and writing tasks they would encounter in the United States. In addition to these competency-oriented materials, students read magazine and newspaper articles on social topics of interest, such as AIDS testing, handgun control, and the English-only movement (Algaier, 1988). Reading for all refugees was given a boost when the program opened community libraries stocked with books on a wide range of subjects.

Cultural Orientation

While ESL helped refugees learn the language they would need in their new communities, cultural orientation provided students with a basic introduction to life and community services in the United States: to sponsorship and resettlement, consumerism, employment, health, and education. Taught primarily in the native language, with the assistance of bilingual refugee aides, cultural orientation classes were also places where students could raise questions and express their concerns.

From U.S. service providers, staff learned what refugees needed to know about life in the United States, and the refugees themselves were full of questions. How the material should be presented was less clear, however. When the cultural orientation curriculum was designed in 1981, there was no extensive field of literature or corps of trained professionals to guide overseas staff. U.S. resettlement communities were providing orientation to refugees, but these sessions were frequently little more than lectures conducted by resettlement workers rather than educators. More innovative pedagogically was the field of intercultural education, but this relatively new discipline had concerned itself with multinational corporate managers, Peace Corps volunteers, foreign students, and other people whose backgrounds and needs were very different from those of Southeast Asian refugees. Refugee families were going to the United States not to study or visit or to have an interesting cross-cultural experience, but to live and to work, perhaps for the rest of their lives. More so than foreign visitors or students, refugees would need to deal with issues of identity, cultural preservation, and change.

Poems from a Refugee Processing Center

Halfway between their past and future lives, the refugee processing centers were places where refugees **remembered their homelands...**

THE LAST SPRING IN MY HOMELAND

TRAN QUANG PHUC

THE SPRING CAME IN MY HOMELAND
ALL THE FLOWERS BLOOMED
BENEATH THE SUNLIGHT.
BUT I FEEL VERY GLOOMY.
BECAUSE THIS IS MY LAST SPRING.
THE LAST SPRING ON MY HOMELAND
TOMORROW I HAVE TO LEAVE.
NOW. HAVING ONLY A FEW MINUTES
OPEN MY HEART TO HOMELAND.

Looking for.
Freedom!
Seeking FREEDOM.
There is death and survive.
Floating on the sea.
During sixteen days.
Alive is seldom.
Death is worth.
Where freedom is
Thy day of seventeenth.
coming freedom.
Where is freedom?
Being caught by the police
puting in prison.
Crying of None reason.
Oh! my ghost! Ham miserable I am!

told of their escapes...

Donald A. Ranard & Margo Pfleger

and anticipated their futures....

HELLO HAPPINESS

NOW I'm here.

what CAN I INAGinE.

THE AirPLANE LAND AT THE AirPOrT.

WHO IN GoinG To kiss first ?

oh! THEre're MY brothers

oh! MY NieCe MY relative

NiNE Years far off

YOU Are GrowinG So tall

SunriSe AND SunSet

Swigtly fly THE YEArs

oh! YoU GeT TO bE A bEAUTY.

AND GrowinG oDEr...

BYE bYE SADNESS

HeIIo HAPPiNESS

oh! weII bE reUNioN.

HeIIo HAPPiNESS...

In the early planning for the cultural orientation component, two approaches emerged. One emphasized basic information about life in the United States. Information, after all, was what refugees said they wanted. They wanted to know how much things cost, what kind of jobs they could get, where they could study English, and where their children would go to school. Information was also what resettlement agencies said that the refugees needed.

A second approach focused on having students examine differences in values and attitudes and develop coping skills. With this approach, students compared and contrasted their own values and attitudes with those of the culture they were about to enter. Before learning about U.S. health care, for example, students discussed health care and medical practices in their own countries. This approach also emphasized cross-cultural coping skills; students learned to observe and imitate, notice and understand cultural differences, as well as to solve problems, make decisions, and use resources in their communities (Redding, 1985).

The effort to find a balance between these two approaches absorbed the energy of cultural orientation staff in the early years of the program. The informational approach could not account for the variety of life in the United States. What was true in Houston was often not true in San Diego. Jobs, cost of living, welfare rates, transportation systems—all varied from place to place. Moreover, the informational approach tended to make the teacher the sole source of knowledge, a role that was inconsistent with learner-centered trends in adult education. Nevertheless, refugees wanted information, and no approach could ignore this basic desire. "We tried to meet felt needs for information as well as to develop analytical and observation skills," noted one cultural orientation specialist (Ranard & Pfleger, 1994).

In dealing with the many changes in their lives, students brought to the classroom a rich repertoire of coping strategies. In the camps and processing centers, they had adapted to new housing, new rules and regulations, and new neighbors. Families had their own adjustments to make, as men took on household responsibilities so that their wives could attend classes. Women became literate and children learned at a faster rate than their parents, upsetting traditional family roles. Through discussion, problem posing, and cooperative learning activities, teachers helped students examine the impact of change on their lives and share strategies for coping with these changes. Over time, the role of the cultural orientation teacher became one of helping learners connect their past and present experiences to their futures. "If the purpose of cultural orientation is to enable the student to adapt to a new set of circumstances," one cultural orientation educator noted, "the educator in a refugee camp has a well-supplied laboratory at his disposal" (Meersman, 1983, p. 13).

Work Orientation

Added to the program in 1983, the work orientation component emphasized the language, cultural knowledge, and basic skills refugees needed to get and keep jobs. Employment had always been an important topic in ESL and cultural orientation classes, but by 1983, there was growing concern that refugees were not adequately prepared for the U.S. workplace. While refugees were generally perceived to be conscientious and productive workers, many lacked sufficient English or knowledge of the U.S. workplace to get, keep, and advance on the job, employers reported (Immigrant and Refugee Planning Center, undated; Latkiewicz, 1981; Literacy 85, 1983).

When work orientation staff first met to design a new curriculum, the field of vocational ESL (VESL) was in an early stage of development. The trend toward teaching language for specific purposes, coupled with growing numbers of newcomers seeking better jobs, had given rise to VESL. This new field comprised two distinct areas: occupation-specific ESL, focusing on the language needed for specific occupations, such as welding and food preparation, and prevocational ESL, emphasizing the general language skills needed for any job (Center for Applied Linguistics, 1983).

The overseas program was in no position to attempt occupation-specific language training during refugees' brief stay in the processing centers. The training period was too short, and refugees' destinations were often not known until a few weeks before their departure. Moreover, job markets in the United States were unpredictable and variable from place to place. For these reasons, work orientation in the overseas program focused on prevocational training.

Work orientation differed from most VESL programs in the United States in that it taught not only ESL but work-related cultural orientation and basic skills, as well. ESL stressed work-related communication, with students learning to use English to ask for clarification, follow and give instructions, obtain more information, and converse socially with co-workers. Cultural orientation provided students with a basic knowledge of the U.S. workplace and an opportunity to compare and contrast Southeast Asian and U.S. workplace customs and practices. Students learned about workplace health and safety, workers' responsibilities and rights, benefits and pay, and opportunities for advancement and further education (International Catholic Migration Commission, 1987). Basic skills focused on job skills such as using diagrams and patterns, computing, and working as part of a team. The importance of this aspect of work orientation training varied with different refugee groups. For refugees from rural backgrounds with little or no formal education, basic skills assumed more importance than it did with those who were better educated.

The three aspects of work orientation—ESL, cultural orientation, and basic skills—were practiced through task-based activities in workplace simulations. At the site in Thailand, silk screening, wood working, electronics, and restaurant activities provided contexts for learning. Students applied their new work orientation skills as they used time cards, gave instructions to a co-worker, practiced workplace safety, and mixed and measured ingredients (Williams, 1986).

In simulated U.S. workplace settings, refugees learned about workplace health and safety and workers' responsibilities and rights.

Native Language Literacy

Though not a core part of the program, native language literacy instruction gradually took hold in Thailand, where large numbers of nonliterate refugees studied. A largely volunteer effort taking place in the evening, the program taught native language literacy, developed reading materials, and ultimately established a resource library. Taught by refugees, the classes served everyone in the family, with women being the predominant population served.

Although in the early years many staff in the overseas program did not understand the relevance of native language literacy to a program preparing refugees for the United States, over time it gained full support. Staff could see for themselves that newly literate refugees faced their futures with more confidence. By the time the Southeast Asia program ends in 1995, more than 30,000 refugees from Vietnam, Laos, and Cambodia will have achieved at least basic literacy. (See Chapter 5 for a description of the native language literacy program.)

Reaching Out to Other Groups

Once a program for adults was solidly in place, staff turned their attention to adults with special needs and to groups who had not been eligible to participate in the program. By 1987, a program that had once limited participation to heads of household was offering special classes to children, mothers, young adults, and refugees with physical or mental disabilities.

Programs for Children

The first major change in the overseas program was the decision to educate refugee children. By 1983, growing numbers of nonliterate Cambodian and Hmong children in the processing centers made staff acutely aware of the special needs of underschooled children.

Reports from U.S. schools contributed to the growing belief that something needed to be done for refugee youth. Entering the United States with little or no previous schooling, many refugee youth were having serious difficulties in their schools and communities. The situation at the secondary level was especially alarming. While elementary school teachers were accustomed to teaching children with no prior classroom experience, secondary school teachers were not; few had been trained in literacy development. Some schools offered intensive ESL programs, but most provided just one or two hours a day of general ESL. During the rest of the day, in their math, history, social studies, and science classes, students would "sink or swim." Many sank (Chung, n.d.). The stereotype of the overachieving Asian valedictorian was being replaced by new stereotypes: the dropout, the gang member, and the teenage mother on welfare.

By late 1984, program planners began the task of recreating in far-off refugee camps the American high school experience. Although the Preparation for American Secondary School (PASS) program began as a simulation of a high school, "anyone walking onto the PASS campus in Bataan would say that, for all practical purposes, it *is* an American high school," reported the first PASS principal in the program in the Philippines.

On what was nothing more than a flat, empty expanse of land . . . there are now nine classroom buildings, an administration building, a library/audio-visual building, and an activities building. There are locker rooms and shower facilities and a sports field for baseball, basketball, soccer, track and field—even bleachers. There is an assembly hall for graduations, school plays, and other programs. We have over 100 staff members, including teachers, education specialists, counselors, curriculum writers, administrative and support staff. . . . During the school day (six 40-minute periods), bells ring between classes, and students move to different classrooms for their various subjects. . . . They get report cards, use hall passes, and get tardy slips from the office. . . . When they act up, they may be sent to the office, where a counselor advises or reprimands them. (Starker, 1986, p. 16)

In determining the instructional content and teaching methodology, PASS planners drew from the growing body of research in bilingual education and second language acquisition. The notion that children acquire a second language through natural interactions rather than through formal study (Dulay, Burt, & Krashen, 1982) argued for a language program rich in natural, authentic language with a focus on communicating real messages for real purposes.

At the same time, students needed help in learning the special kind of English needed to succeed in school. Researchers were making a distinction between two types of language proficiency (Cummins, 1981). One kind, social language—the language of face-to-face communication—was acquired in a relatively short period of time through social interaction. Academic language— the more formal, decontextualized language of textbooks and the classroom—took much longer to learn. Students would need to develop both types of proficiency.

These and other developments profoundly affected the PASS curriculum. An English-rich environment would promote acquisition.

At the same time, students' limited prior schooling meant that they also needed exposure to basic information and concepts in traditional school subjects. What emerged was a PASS curriculum comprising three components: English language arts, which developed both oral skills and reading and writing; social studies, focusing on history and geography; and basic science and math, with an emphasis on discovery and problem solving. Refugee teacher aides provided bilingual support.

Many of the PASS students came to school with little confidence in their ability to learn and with little experience interacting with their peers in a classroom setting. To help students gain confidence and develop interpersonal skills, PASS initiated an activity-based counseling program in which students worked as a group to perform physically and mentally challenging tasks. To meet students' individual needs, bilingual counselors, many of them former refugees, helped students sort out problems at school and at home.

Extending educational opportunities to children of elementary school age followed naturally on the heels of PASS. By 1987, primary-school children were included in a program called PREP, Preparing Refugees for Elementary Programs. Although younger children were not as seriously at risk in U.S. schools as their older counterparts, a head start in English language and literacy development helped them enter elementary school with basic comprehension skills and subject matter knowledge.

In PREP, English was taught through content areas such as reading, writing, math, science, art, and drama. Students were allowed to progress naturally through the stages of language acquisition, using nonverbal responses and unconventional spelling in the beginning, and later, developing fluency through language experience activities and cooperative learning tasks (Hoyt, 1993).

Because program designers believed that children develop fluency most readily when they have a need to express themselves (Corey, Hamayan, & Pfleger, 1987), teachers linked language to real experience. Students made animal habitats, acted out folktales, and conducted science experiments. New vocabulary and structures were introduced in the context of the activity, and students began using the target language before they had fully mastered its form (Hoyt, 1993).

Literacy instruction in PREP was simultaneous with oral language development. Through whole language approaches such as language experience stories, shared reading with big books, dictated stories, and dialogue journals, children read and wrote about familiar themes and topics. Students were encouraged to use their native language and personal histories to connect what they knew with what they were learning (Hoyt, 1993).

As staff became more familiar with their students' personal histories—through student writings as well as through visits to students' homes—they became aware of the contributions that families could make to their children's education. Through homework assignments that involved the whole family and through parent participation in the classroom, teachers built a partnership between the school and home. (See Chapter 6 for a description of this aspect of PREP.)

Even preschoolers were part of the overseas training program. Modeled on Project Head Start, a childcare program in Thailand provided young children with good nutrition and activities that stimulated early development.

Special Needs Groups: Women, Young Adults, and Refugees with Disabilities

Refugee education emerged as a separate discipline when educators realized that refugees had educational needs that were different from those of other ESL learners. Soon the field recognized that the refugee population itself was not homogeneous; it included groups with distinct needs based on different backgrounds and resettlement experiences. Guided by surveys and other sources of information from U.S. service providers, the overseas program began designing curricula for two special-needs groups: mothers and young adults. Special courses were also designed for individuals with physical and mental disabilities.

Women

In its first few years, the overseas program had given primary attention to the male head of household. By the early 1980s, there was growing evidence of the critical role in resettlement that women played, as well. A family's successful integration depended to a large degree on the adjustment of women (Lutheran Immigration and Refugee Service, n.d.), who maintained the home and raised the children. Yet women, particularly those with young children, faced special difficulties. A host of conditions—limited English, unfamiliarity with Western home management, and the rapid acculturation of children into U.S. culture—undermined women's traditional role as family caregivers. At the same time, responsibilities at home kept them from learning new skills they needed to assume new roles and responsibilities. Isolated at home, many women slipped into depression, feeling that they were not contributing to their families' well-being. A special report to the overseas program on the resettlement experiences of women noted that women's "isolation and homebound status . . . encourage dependency and compound the issues of adjustment, within their own family and their community" (Mackintosh, 1985, p. 2).

To prepare new mothers for the stresses they would face in the United States, the overseas program designed a course for pregnant women and those with young children. A supplement to the regular adult curriculum, the course was intended to help these women develop "the skills . . . to function in the family and the community" (International Catholic Migration Commission, 1985, p. 7). The course began with the recognition that many women with young children would not be able to work outside the home: "In their present condition, they may . . . stay at home and be [homemakers] rather than seek employment" (International Catholic Migration Commission, 1985, p. 20). The new topics, taught mostly in the native language with the assistance of refugee aides, included day care, health care during pregnancy and post partum, child development, consumerism, household safety, nutrition, and

Young adult refugees spent four hours per day in the classroom, but pursued their studies independently in their living quarters when class ended.

community services. Students also learned about home-based employment opportunities, such as sewing, that would allow them to contribute to the family income (Turetsky, Bustard, & Rattanakom, 1988).

Young Adults

Another portion of the adult population to receive special attention was young adults. The challenge of entering a new culture was especially daunting for young adults, forced to negotiate an unfamiliar culture at the same time they were grappling with many first-time life experiences—getting and keeping a job, dating, getting married, having a family (M. Webster in Forum: Refugee Youth, 1986). Guided by the results of a survey (Center for Applied Linguistics, 1988), the overseas program designed a supplemental course of study for young adults. Because most young adult refugees wanted to continue their education, yet often needed to work, the course gave particular attention to strategies for working and studying at the same time. In their work orientation classes, young adults learned basic math, and in ESL classes, they learned the language needed "to succeed in educational situations [and] . . . to access information regarding [job] skills development and certification" (Gilzow, 1988, p. 46). Through role plays, case studies, and debates, students in cultural orientation classes explored social issues of special interest, such as dating, marriage, and peer pressure.

The young adult program in the Philippines grew in scope and complexity with the arrival in the late 1980s of large numbers of Vietnamese Amerasians. Though in their late teens, most had received only a few years of education in Vietnam. Having grown up on the social and economic margins of Vietnamese society, many arrived with low self-esteem and without the support of a stable family. To meet the pressing needs of these young adults, the program developed a wide range of academic, social, and recreational activities. The cultural orientation curriculum was reconfigured to pay more attention to issues of self, family, and community. Students examined personal qualities, explored family roles, looked at their place within the community and society, and discussed their hopes and plans for the future.

Outside the classroom, Amerasians developed their social skills through participation in sports and social clubs and explored issues of interest in informal discussion groups. Topics of discrimination, always a subject of interest to refugees, took on special meaning with this mixed-race population. For example, through activities on Black history and culture, Black Amerasians drew parallels between the African-American experience and their experience growing up in Vietnam. Vietnamese-American counselors helped students resolve problems in their classroom and neighborhoods. (See Chapter 4 for a description of the young adult program.)

Refugees with Disabilities

Like other populations, the refugee population included those with physical, mental, and emotional disabilities. To meet the needs of these learners, the program in Thailand designed what became known as the Super-A program. Since most Super-A students entered the program with little or no English or literacy in their native language, the Super-A course generally followed the A-level curriculum for nonliterate beginners, but with a focus on topics of particular importance to refugees with disabilities. Students learned how to communicate information about themselves and to handle emergencies. Deaf students studied sign language—International Sign Language in the beginning years, American Sign Language in recent years. Slow learners studied lessons suited to their needs and learning styles. Super-A teachers approached topics in a variety of ways, using the senses of sight, hearing, and touch to draw on students' strengths (Super-A Program Staff, 1986).

Bringing Learners Together

Once the overseas program had developed curricula to meet the needs of different age groups—adults, young adults, and children—it began looking at ways of bringing learners together to interact and support one another. One approach used the family as a resource, because it built upon the backgrounds of the learners. Southeast Asian refugees came from cultures where the family, rather than the individual, was the basic unit of society (Ranard, 1989), and in the process of adjusting to a new culture, families often played a critical role, with family members working cooperatively to overcome obstacles (Rumbaut & Ima, 1987). At the same time, refugee families were at risk for intergenerational conflict, with children and parents adapting to the new culture at different rates and in different ways.

Learning activities brought together adults, young adults, and adolescents to share viewpoints and experiences. Special discussion groups provided parents and young adults a safe place to discuss issues, such as dating and changing family roles, that might lead to family conflicts in the United States. To strengthen parents' roles as teachers, adults visited children's classes to demonstrate traditional skills and to talk about their lives in their native countries. Homework assignments were designed to use parents as sources of knowledge; one assignment had students interview parents about their past experiences. Through special events, the program sought to promote family interaction and strengthen intergenerational ties. At family fairs, families read books together, performed skits, played games, and told stories. During family appreciation night, young adults demonstrated skills they had learned in their classes.

Many young refugees arrived in the camps without the support of stable families. For these refugees, the program looked to the community for intergenerational support. Older students worked with young adults on projects such as tree planting, gardening, and electrical repair. Through interest clubs, young and older adults pursued interests in photography, music, and art. A big brother/sister program provided young adults with support and guidance through friendship with camp staff.

Learning from Each Other: Trends in Staff Development

Teachers in the overseas program—Indonesian, Thai, and Filipino nationals—were college graduates, highly proficient in English. Assisting teachers in the classroom were refugees with advanced-level English, while language and cross-cultural specialists and program administrators provided instructional support. In the early years of the program, almost all nonteaching positions were held by Americans, but eventually former refugees were employed in key positions, such as cross-cultural specialists and counselors. Over time, as non-American staff gained experience and expertise, they became specialists and managers, as well. By 1995, most positions throughout the program were held by Filipino and Thai nationals.

While many teachers had backgrounds in education, few had been trained in learner-centered approaches. To train teachers in current theory and practice, the program initiated the team approach to staff development. In small groups led by language and cross-cultural specialists, teachers met 10 to 15 hours a week to plan lessons, discuss issues, and share strategies.

As the instructional program changed to reflect new trends in refugee education, so too did staff development change to reflect

As the program ends in 1995, thousands of Filipino, Thai, and Indonesian teachers of language and culture have become seasoned professionals.

new ideas in teacher education. To meet the diverse needs and interests of the teaching staff, the program expanded opportunities for professional development. At one site, the program came to resemble a teacher-training institute with dozens of courses on second language acquisition and cross-cultural education. Through ties the program had established with local teacher training colleges, teachers could even earn graduate degrees while teaching in the camp.

By the mid-1980s, staff in the Philippines were exchanging ideas in an annual, camp-wide conference on language and culture; topics ranged from refugee gangs in America to traditional Southeast Asian healing practices to strategies for independent learning (International Catholic Migration Commission, 1993). A steady stream of consultants from the United States kept staff abreast of new developments in the field. Two publications, *Information Update* and *In America,* were developed to provide staff with up-to-date information on refugee resettlement trends and issues. Through the program's own publication, *Passage: A Journal of Refugee Education,* staff exchanged information and ideas among colleagues, both in the overseas program and in refugee programs in the United States.

The refugees themselves also provided rich opportunities for staff development. As part of preservice training, new staff participated in a "homestay"—a day with a refugee family. By spending time with a family at school, at work, and at home, staff saw the camp through the refugees' eyes (Marston, 1986). Staff could also take classes in Southeast Asian languages. Taught by refugees, these classes not only gave staff another means of communicating with their students, they also helped teachers "appreciate the pleasures and difficulties [their] own students encounter[ed]" (Duffy & MacArthur, 1985, p. 10).

Paralleling the growth of learner-centered trends in the classroom, staff development became increasingly self-directed. Through observing peers, reading professional journals, conducting classroom-based research, or presenting at workshops, teachers began assuming responsibility for their own learning. Rather than participating in a predetermined schedule of training classes, teachers selected from a menu of training opportunities and planned their own professional development.

As the program ends in 1995, thousands of Indonesian, Thai, and Filipino teachers have become experienced language and cross-cultural educators. Many have returned to teach in their home towns and provinces, taking with them new ideas and practices about education. Some have started their own schools. Others have used skills they acquired in the program to begin new careers, many as staff development trainers in hotels and companies (Consortium, 1995). Thus, the significance of the program can be measured by its impact not only on the refugees but on the host countries as well.

Conclusion

Throughout its history, the overseas program was part of the larger field of refugee and immigrant education. Staff were hired from programs and schools in the United States, bringing with them new ideas and practices. Countless consultants contributed their expertise. The result was a program where the latest ideas in

Significance of Setting

Far-off refugee camps might seem unlikely places to prepare refugees for life in America, but staff soon discovered the unique opportunities for exploring issues of culture and change that the program's multicultural milieu offered. Halfway between the old country and the new, the camps were also places where refugees could begin to sort out past experiences—sometimes deeply painful experiences—and prepare for future challenges.

With this setting came another benefit, as American staff discovered the special strengths and skills that non-native speakers brought to the class-room. Who could better understand the difficulties of learning English than Thai, Filipino, and Indonesian teachers who themselves had once struggled to learn the language? The bond between teacher and learner can be especially close when they share a language and culture, as was often the case in the overseas program.

Setting—and a management philosophy that supported experimentation—also contributed to change. As one former staff person noted, "Bring creative people together in a refugee camp, where there's not much to do except work, and you're going to get a lot of innovation" (K. Corey, personal communication, March 1994).

language and cross-cultural education were proposed, debated, and tested.

In early 1995, as the last students prepared to graduate from the Southeast Asia program, staff could look back on a decade and a half of almost constant change and experimentation. The program's original purpose—to help ease refugees' transition into a new culture—remained the same. But over time, the program grew enormously in scope, design, and complexity, as it continually redefined what it considered essential for survival. While competency-based curricula retained critical importance in the program, they became part of a more ambitious effort to meet a wide range of educational and pyschosocial needs. Classroom instruction paid more attention to learners' need for literacy. Learning occurred not only in the classroom, but also in neighborhood libraries, in multimedia resource centers, on recreation fields, and at home.

Counselors, some of them former refugees themselves, served as bridges between school, home, and community. The program reached out to new groups, designing special courses for children, adolescents, young adults, and women. Once the needs of different groups were met, the program sought to bring refugees of all ages together through activities that strengthened intergenerational and family ties.

Although the program in Southeast Asia is ending, it leaves a lasting legacy. The success of the Southeast Asian programs has led the U.S. Department of State to fund similar though smaller-scale efforts in Kenya and in Croatia for U.S.-bound African and Bosnian refugees. In the United States, the overseas program's competency-based curriculum remains a model for refugee education programs, as well as for other language education efforts: Peace Corps, for example, redesigned its language training programs for volunteers in the late 1980s, using the overseas program's ESL curriculum as a model. The overseas program's efforts in cultural orientation have contributed to the burgeoning field of cross-cultural education, as former staff bring new ideas to their work in the public, private, and nonprofit sectors. Because of the large number of nonliterate refugees who studied in the program, literacy was a particularly fruitful area of work, and the program has left behind a rich resource of student- and teacher-created materials that are now used in ESL programs throughout the United States. The program's work with refugee youth has also contributed to the field's knowledge about how best to educate children in a second language.

Other initiatives have been less well publicized. Three of these efforts—a native language literacy program, a partnership between school and families, and a program for underschooled young adults—represent areas of lively interest in the field today. They are treated in detail in the following chapters in the hope that in these areas, too, the overseas program can provide useful ideas to educators seeking new ways to help newcomers make the most of their new lives in America.

References

Aguilar, H., Blackstock, A., Mauricio, L., Snyder, S., & Walsh, S. (1988, Spring & Summer). The ESL-A/B book project. *Passage: A Journal of Refugee Education, 4*(1&2), 63-70.

Algaier, C. (1988, Spring & Summer). Meeting the needs of upper-level ESL students at Bataan. *Passage: A Journal of Refugee Education, 4*(1&2), 80-82.

Center for Applied Linguistics. (1983). *From the classroom to the workplace: Teaching ESL to adults.* Washington, DC: Author.

Center for Applied Linguistics. (1988, January). *Young adult refugee survey: Final report. Prepared for the Bureau for Refugee Programs, U.S. Department of State.* Washington, DC: Author.

Chung, C.H. (n.d.). *Working with Vietnamese high school students.* Unpublished manuscript, New Faces of Liberty, Berkeley, CA.

Consortium. (1995). *Survey of former Consortium staff members.* Unpublished manuscript, the Consortium, Bangkok, Thailand.

Corey, K.M. (1986, Spring). ESL curriculum development in the overseas refugee training program: A personal account. *Passage: A Journal of Refugee Education, 2*(1), 5-11.

Corey, K., Hamayan, E.V., & Pfleger, M. (1987, September). A whole language program for refugee children. *ERIC/CLL News Bulletin 11*(1), 1, 4-6, 7.

Cummins, J.E. (1981). The role of primary language development in promoting educational success for language minority students. In *Schooling and language minority students: A theoretical framework.* Los Angeles: California State University; Education, Dissemination and Assessment Center.

Duffy, J.M., & MacArthur, C. (1985, Winter/Spring). Studying refugees' languages: A new approach in staff development. *Passage: A Journal of Refugee Education, 1*(1), 9-12.

Dulay, H., Burt, M., & Krashen, S. (1982). *Language two*. New York: Oxford University Press.

Forum: Refugee youth. (1986, Spring). *Passage: A Journal of Refugee Education, 2*(1), 38-49.

Gilzow, D.F. (1988, Spring & Summer). New focus on young adult refugees in the overseas program. *Passage: A Journal of Refugee Education, 4*(1&2), 44-46.

Hiponia, M., & Walker, D. (1983, March). The ESL/CO integrated curriculum: An illustrated history. *The Journal: A Publication for English as a Second Language and Cultural Orientation Teachers, 2*(1), 3-11.

Hoyt, L. (1993). How do they learn to read and write? Literacy instruction in a refugee camp. In K.D. Samway & D. McKeon (Eds.), *Common threads of practice: Teaching English to children around the world* (pp. 67-77). Alexandria, VA: Teachers of English to Speakers of Other Languages.

Immigrant and Refugee Planning Center. (n.d.). *Capturing the change: The impact of Indochinese refugees in Orange County: Challenges and opportunities*. Santa Ana, CA: Author.

International Catholic Migration Commission. (1985). Bataan program design review recommendations as of 11 October 1985. In *Regional design review, fall 1985*. Unpublished pre-conference papers, Center for Applied Linguistics, Washington DC.

International Catholic Migration Commission. (1987). *The work orientation syllabus*. Morong, Bataan, Philippines: Author.

International Catholic Migration Commission. (1993). *BCLC '93: Bridges and gateways. Program guide for the Bataan conference on language and culture*. Bataan, Philippines: Author.

Kharde, L.S., & Corey, K. (1986, Summer). Competencies revisited: Revising the overseas ESL curriculum. *Passage: A Journal of Refugee Education, 2*(2), 43-49.

Kuntz, L. (1982). *The new arrival: ESL stories for ESL students, book one*. San Francisco, CA: Alemany.

Larsen-Freeman, D. (1986). *Techniques and principles in language teaching.* New York: Oxford University Press.

Latkiewicz, J. (1981). *Industry's reaction to the Indochinese.* Salt Lake City, UT: Technical College, Skills Center.

Literacy 85. (1983, March 31). *ESL/employment survey: Job related problems identified by employers of Indochinese.* St. Paul, MN: Author.

Lutheran Immigration and Refugee Service. (n.d.). *One year after arrival: The adjustment of Indochinese women in the United States, 1979-1980.* New York, NY: Author.

Mackintosh, W.T. (1985), *A-B level students: Resettlement experiences and stateside services for caretakers* (2nd draft). Unpublished manuscript, Center for Applied Linguistics, Washington, DC.

Marston, J. (1986, Summer). Homestay. *Passage: A Journal of Refugee Education, 2*(2), 64-66.

Meersman, T. (1983, March). A laboratory guide for C[ultural] O[rientation]. *The Journal: A Publication for English as a Second Language and Cultural Orientation Teachers, 2*(1), 12-15.

Ranard, D.A., (1989, December). Family literacy: Trends & practices. *In America: Perspectives on Refugee Resettlement, 7,* 1-4.

Ranard, D.A., & Pfleger, M. (1994). *Reflections on educating refugees: Interviews with staff of the overseas refugee training program.* Unpublished manuscript, Center for Applied Linguistics, Washington, DC.

Redding, J.P. (1985, Summer). Cultural orientation at Bataan: Merging trends. *Passage: A Journal of Refugee Education, 1*(2), 22-26.

Riddle, T. (1985). *Writing back: Letters from Indochinese refugees in the U.S.* Phanat Nikhom, Thailand: The Consortium.

Rumbaut, R.G., & Ima, K. (1987). *The adaptation of Southeast Asian refugee youth: A comparative study.* Washington, DC: U.S. Government Printing Office.

Starker, G. (1986, Spring). Preparing refugee youth for the U.S. at the Philippine Refugee Processing Center. *Passage: A Journal of Refugee Education, 2*(1), 16-19.

Super-A Program Staff. (1986, Summer). The super-A program: Assisting refugees with special needs. *Passage: A Journal of Refugee Education, 2*(2), 62-63.

Turetsky, A., Bustard, L., & Rattanakom, S. (1988, Spring & Summer). The learning center in Phanat Nikhom. *Passage: A Journal of Refugee Education, 4*(1&2), 9-12.

Turner, H., Ligon, F., DiGregorio, M., LaMare, H., & Hicks, J. (1989). *From their side: Young adult refugees in the U.S., a teacher resource.* Bangkok, Thailand: The Consortium and the International Catholic Migration Commission.

Wallerstein, N. (1983, October). Problem-posing can help students learn: From refugee camps to resettlement country classrooms. *TESOL Newsletter,* pp. 28-30.

Wheeler, J. (1986, Winter). Clinic simulation. *Passage: A Journal of Refugee Education, 2*(3), 18-20.

Williams, G. (1986, Winter). The D-E work orientation pilot program in Phanat Nikhom. *Passage: A Journal of Refugee Education, 2*(3), 6-9.

Chapter Four
Beyond the Classroom

John Michael Phillips

Beyond the Classroom

Meeting the Needs of Young Adult Amerasians

John Michael Phillips
International Catholic Migration Commission
Philippine Refugee Processing Center

Sitting on low wooden benches under the shade of a spreading mango tree, Khuyen sips coffee and listens to three young Vietnamese students talk about their frustrations with learning English. Khuyen, a counselor, suggested the meeting at the local coffee shop after a heated exchange between a teacher and one of the students earlier that morning. The student, Khai, a tough-looking 20-year-old Vietnamese-Amerasian, complains that his teacher is against him. Another, 19-year-old Toan, who left Vietnam six years ago by boat and has no relatives in camp, despairs of making any progress in learning English. The third student, an Afro-Amerasian named Michael, says he can't concentrate in class because of problems he is having at home with his stepfather. "Uncle" Khuyen, as he is known to students, nods, making a mental note to pay a visit to Michael's house later in the week. When Khuyen finally speaks, it is not to give advice, but to help the students sort out the reasons for their difficulties. Khuyen has been working with young people for several years and knows he cannot solve their problems, but he can help them look at their situations and find their own solutions.

Pham Khuyen worked as a counselor in the young adult program at the Philippine Refugee Processing Center (PRPC). Like the other counselors, Khuyen was a bilingual Vietnamese-American with experience in social work and education. He and his colleagues, all former refugees, formed one part of a comprehensive program for young adult refugees, many of whom were Amerasians from Vietnam.

From 1987 until the overseas program in the Philippines closed in 1994, the young adult program provided services to more than 25,000 refugees between the ages of 17 and 25. Implemented by the International Catholic Migration Commission (ICMC), the young adult program was founded on the belief that young adults, particularly Vietnamese Amerasians with low levels of education and personal histories of discrimination and family conflict, had both academic and psychosocial needs. To meet these needs, the program moved beyond traditional classroom instruction to provide a wide range of academic, social, recreational, and counseling services. Attending ESL, literacy, and cultural orientation classes during the day and taikwando, cosmetology, and native language literacy classes in the evening, students benefited from a full program of academic study and social recreation. On weekends, they joined in youth club activities, spent the day with a big sister or brother, or took part in informal discussion groups exploring issues of interest to young adults. Vietnamese-speaking counselors were never far from the refugees' neighborhoods, keeping tabs on troubled youth or visiting with families, often doing on-the-spot counseling and crisis intervention.

Rationale and History

By 1990, most of the students in the young adult program were Amerasians and their siblings, but when the program began in 1987, Amerasians from Vietnam were only a small portion of the young adult population. Serving mostly non-Amerasian Vietnamese youth, the young adult program was initiated to assist refugees between the ages of 17 and 22. These young adult migrants faced a daunting and distinctive set of challenges in the United States: Almost all would be working, some for the first time; many would also be going to school. At the same time, most would be dating, getting married, and starting new families (Center for Applied Linguistics, 1988). Many would be facing the resettlement experience without the support of family or close friends.

About 15% of Amerasians have African-American fathers. Only a small number of all Amerasians have reunited with their fathers in America.

The purpose of the young adult curriculum was to prepare students to face new life experiences and make informed choices (Gilzow, 1988). Classroom activities helped students get information about educational and employment options in their new communities and develop strategies for working and studying at the same time. Like adult students, young adults studied ESL, cultural orientation, and work orientation, but in each case the instructional content was adjusted to the special needs of young adults. In work orientation classes, for example, students with little previous education learned math; in cultural orientation classes they discussed young adult issues, such as male/female relationships and peer pressure; and in ESL classes, they practiced social language.

When large numbers of Amerasians arrived from Vietnam in 1989, nearly all entered the young adult program. Most shared many interests and concerns with other refugees their age. At the same time, it soon became clear that many Amerasians brought with them needs that set them apart from other young adults. Offspring of servicemen and other Americans who had served in Vietnam during the 1960s and 1970s, many Amerasians had grown up in poverty on the social and economic fringes of Vietnamese society. Most had attended school for only two or three years.

Some could not read or write Vietnamese and had little or no experience in an academic learning environment.

Their difficulties were not just academic. Having grown up different in a society that valued uniformity, many Amerasians were also grappling with issues of identity and discrimination. Because Vietnam is a patriarchal society in which one's identity is linked to one's father, many Amerasians had a poorly formed sense of self (Blundell, 1985; Ronk, 1986). Moreover, the Vietnamese government and many Vietnamese people regarded Amerasians as tainted by American blood. To many, Amerasians represented the hated, vanquished enemy and were often used as "bad" examples in school lessons about the war. The widespread (though inaccurate) perception among Vietnamese that most mothers of Amerasians were prostitutes further marginalized them.

In addition, Amerasians' family circumstances often led to serious problems. Many had come to the processing center unaccompanied by family members, while others had rejoined their families, after many years of separation, for the purpose of resettlement. In some instances, Amerasians were living with fraudulent "family" members—people who had paid Amerasians or their mothers to let them impersonate a family member for the purpose of emigrating with the Amerasian to the United States. In these cases, Amerasians were living with virtual strangers, sometimes hostile ones, and the result sometimes involved abuse.

Not all Amerasians fit this at-risk profile. Some were high school graduates who had grown up in stable, loving families and seemed happy and well adjusted. Nonetheless, the majority of Amerasians had special educational and psychosocial needs, and the effort to meet these needs ultimately led to sweeping changes in the young adult program, both inside and outside the classroom.

Inside the Classroom

For many Amerasians, school in Vietnam had been a place of failure. As a result, they tended to see education, even education for resettlement, as not worth the effort. If the overseas program was to succeed where other educational efforts had failed, it would need to engage Amerasians and help them gain confidence in their own capacity to learn.

Guided by the principle that students learn best when what they learn interests them, program staff adapted curricula and materials to the interests of Amerasians. Cultural orientation classes emphasized such issues as peer pressure, discrimination, and dating, while in their ESL classes students read stories with Amerasian characters. The ESL department transformed the language laboratory into a multimedia learning resource center, with materials reflecting the backgrounds and interests of young adult students. Students read and then discussed open-ended young adult stories, such as "Will Stacie Keep Her Baby?" They wrote reactions to videos about Vietnam and listened to audiotapes of readings, with supplementary illustrated texts, on young adult topics. A bulletin board invited students to respond to controversial statements or to conflicting proverbs.

One way to ensure student interest is to offer students choice in what they study. Reflecting trends in refugee and immigrant education (Wrigley & Guth, 1992), the ESL classroom became a more democratic place, with students and teachers collaboratively deciding on topics for study (Snyder, 1990). At the beginning ESL levels, an experimental whole-language literacy program encouraged self-directed learning. Students not only studied prescribed lifeskill topics, such as reading ads and filling out forms; they also carried out high-interest activities, such as reporting neighborhood events to the class, reading books on topics of interest, and writing personal stories.

In cultural orientation classes, students had the opportunity to choose both course content and approach. Students also directed their own learning through specific activities such as Special Projects and Learn-A-Skill. With Special Projects, students launched large-scale projects, such as sports tournaments, cultural shows, field trips, and dance parties, and in the process learned goal-setting and planning skills. Students worked on their projects in groups, an especially effective approach with underschooled students reluctant to perform in front of others: A young adult too shy to stand before the entire class would participate confidently in an informal discussion among four or five peers. With Learn-A-Skill, students developed new skills that could be as simple as throwing a frisbee or as complex as playing chess. Other choices included modern dance, hairdressing, baseball, and painting. The emphasis was on gaining self-confidence as well as on skills that would provide a contact point for socialization with American young adults. Students learned and practiced the skills outside class but were responsible for periodic in-class progress reports and demonstrations.

Students even had a say in how their classrooms were run. Many young adults came to the program with little or no classroom experience. Some acted inappropriately because they did not know how they were expected to behave. Others acted out, masking a fear of failure. One particularly effective way of dealing with an unruly classroom, teachers discovered, was to let students develop their own classroom rules: Students were more likely to obey rules that they themselves had made. To set classroom rules, students might begin by talking about rules at home and in the camp. In one lesson, for example, the teacher would show students a picture of camp living quarters. "How do you get along when you are living so close together?" the teacher would ask, leading to a discussion of how refugees solved problems that came from living with others in the camp. This discussion, in turn, would lead to a list of rules that refugees follow to get along with their new neighbors. Then, students and teacher would work together to develop a list of rules for classroom behavior.

Gai is an Amerasian. Her mother is Vietnamese. Her father was an American soldier. When the war ended, Gai's father went home. Gai and her mother were left alone.

They had no money, so they sold cakes on the streets. Gai was still very small, and she was always tired and hungry. Life in Vietnam was too difficult for Gai and her mother, so they left.

Now they are in the PRPC, waiting to go to America. But Gai is worried. She looks like an American, but she cannot speak English.

How can she make friends? The Vietnamese think she is American; the Americans think she is Vietnamese. Gai is afraid that life in America will be difficult too.

From *Gai*, a staff-developed storybook by Alan Blackstock and Mario C. Hernandez produced by the International Catholic Migration Commission, Philippine Refugee Processing Center, Morong, Bataan, Philippines, 1988.

In a further effort to help Amerasians become more responsible for their own learning, ESL classes incorporated strategies for continuing learning. Designed to help students become independent, lifelong learners, these strategies appeared throughout the ESL curriculum. In a unit dealing with shopping for food, for example, students would "find out prices of basic food items" in the camp markets and then "report the information and write it down, comparing item, price, place, day, and quality." Lessons like this helped students go beyond mastery of specific information to develop skills they could use in the United States to get information independently.

Applying information-gathering strategies on a larger scale, ESL students undertook long-term research projects. First, students chose a topic that interested them; the topic might reflect a resettlement concern (e.g., occupations in the United States), a social issue (e.g., the African-American experience), or a personal interest (e.g., Chinese cooking). Then, working with others with similar interests, students identified sources of information, developed a plan for carrying out their research, and organized a presentation of their findings to the class (International Catholic Migration Commission, 1989).

Outside the Classroom

Effective as these classroom innovations were, many Amerasians and other young adults needed more than language and cultural instruction. Energetic young adults not used to spending long hours in a classroom needed the stimulation of social and recreational activities, while others needed help with family and personal problems.

The field of language education has supported the idea that social services can contribute to better language acquisition (Kleinmann, 1982). Language students do not learn as well when they are anxious or depressed, ESL educators believe (Krashen & Terrell, 1983; Schumann, 1980). One way to reduce stress and facilitate learning is to create a low-anxiety learning environment where students are encouraged to take risks and express their ideas, desires, and feelings (Cohon, Lucey, Paul, & Penning, 1986). Another way is to provide "professional social services to alleviate pressing needs and overwhelming stresses" (Kleinmann, 1982, p. 241). Social services, Robinson (1980) argues, represent "one of the strongest defenses against depression and mental stresses among refugees" (p. 35).

At the Philippine Refugee Processing Center, the need for support services outside the classroom led to the creation of a comprehensive program of social and recreational activities. In addition, a special counseling unit made up of bilingual Vietnamese-American counselors was formed.

Social and Recreational Activities

Social and recreational activities were organized and led by staff of the Young Adult Services Program (YASP). Through the recreational side of the program, students learned to sew, box, cook, or play the guitar. Basketball, volleyball, and American football games

Social and recreational activities were an important part of the comprehensive program developed to assist young adult refugees.

were organized, as well as classes in acting, singing, drawing, and martial arts. It was hoped that these activities—along with English language skills—might provide an entree to new friendships in the United States. As YASP Coordinator Roger Kern explained,

When students go to America, the first people they are actually going to socialize with are other young people, and the way they are going to do that is at dances, basketball games, and other recreational activities. If they know how to do these activities, they will be able to develop friendships. (Ranard & Pfleger, 1994)

There was a serious purpose to these activities, as well. As a psychologist who worked closely with Amerasians at the camp in the Philippines and in the United States notes, "In general, the source of competence and self-esteem for most Amerasians has not been rooted in the classroom" (Felsman, Johnson, Frederick, & Felsman, 1989, p. 50). This observation suggests that many underschooled young adults would be more likely to gain new skills and confidence on the playing field or in a social club than in the classroom.

One example of the educational value of recreation was the "ropes course." Despite a superficial resemblance to an obstacle course, the ropes course was far more sophisticated than a simple fitness activity. Designed to build confidence, trust, and self-awareness, the course required students to engage in physically and mentally challenging activities. There were several benefits to the course. As students helped one another cross a bridge made of rope or caught someone in a free fall, they learned in a very concrete way the value of cooperation and trust. For students who had experienced little but isolation and failure in Vietnam, the course helped develop confidence and friendship. And, finally, because each activity was followed by a discussion period that allowed participants to talk about how they felt and what they had learned, there was a context for discussing issues that otherwise might be neglected. "They can talk about fear and the value of trust and cooperation because they've just experienced it," says Michael Conway, a San Francisco policeman who worked with at-risk youth in San Francisco and served as a consultant to the young adult program (Ranard & Pfleger, 1994). Also known as activity-based counseling, the ropes course proved especially effective with young people who did not benefit from traditional approaches to counseling (Ong, 1992).

In addition to recreational activities, YASP provided an array of social services. Through its Big Brother/Big Sister program, staff volunteers offered guidance and even friendship to young adults, especially those without relatives in camp. On Sundays, Americans working in the camp met with Amerasians for casual talks and recreation. Field trips to schools and residential and commercial areas on nearby military bases gave Amerasians the chance to see, first hand, aspects of American life they had studied in their cultural orientation classes and to play sports with Americans (International Catholic Migration Commission, 1989).

The program also brought together young adults with similar interests. Special-interest support groups, such as the Afro-Amerasian Rap Group and the Women's Club, met on weekends. The rap group discussed issues such as racism, discrimination, and identity, while the Women's Club addressed issues of self-esteem and gender. At times, the two groups' interests merged. There were joint sessions, for example, that helped young Afro-

One assumption underlying activities for underschooled young adults was that they would be more likely to gain new skills and confidence on the playing field or in a social club than in the classroom.

Amerasian women develop pride in their appearance as they learned about hair care and received tips on makeup—an important step, since Afro-Amerasians had been particularly stigmatized in Vietnam (Ranard & Gilzow, 1989).

The Young Adult Services Program also offered special English classes for newly arrived refugees still waiting for their classes to begin. Taught by bilingual teachers, these classes gave underschooled young adults an opportunity to experience and understand the classroom environment. A variety of other course topics, such as Vietnamese literacy, were also offered, depending on student interest and the availability of volunteer teachers.

Counseling

A critical element of the young adult program was the counseling unit, known as the Young Adult Services Unit (YASU). YASU advisers—all Vietnamese-Americans, all former refugees—linked the staff with the students, and the classroom with the community. Operating in the neighborhoods, the classrooms, and the recreational facilities, YASU advisers provided refugees with orientation to camp life and the curriculum, counseled troubled students one-on-one, and helped resolve conflicts among refugees and between students and staff. With students who entered the program with little or no education, an important part of the advisers' job was to help them see that they were capable of learning. As one adviser noted,

When they first arrive, they always say, "Oh, I am from the rural area or the mountain area and stupid. I cannot speak English." So we teach them a few simple words or phrases each day, and soon they see that they are learning. Or a student has been studying for a while and says he can't learn anything, so we sit down with him and look at his notebook or speak some English with him and say, "See, you have learned a lot." (Ranard & Pfleger, 1994)

The key to the advisers' success was the culture and language they shared with the students. As former refugees themselves, advisers brought to their work a firsthand knowledge of U.S. resettlement realities as well as an understanding of Vietnamese and American cultures. Speaking to a group of Americans, an adviser made this point: "If you were a refugee in a camp and were going to Iran, who would you listen to more—an Iranian or another American who had lived in Iran? The Iranian would know more about Iran, but the American speaks your language and has had the experience you're going to have. If you put yourself in the shoes of the refugee, I think you'll see why a Vietnamese here is going to listen to another refugee" (Ranard & Pfleger, 1994).

YASU advisers also needed to recognize when to make referrals to Community Family Services Incorporated (CFSI), the agency that provided bilingual and bicultural mental health services to refugees in the camp. The relationship between YASU advisers and the more formally trained staff at CFSI was a crucial one and led to linkages with elementary school programs, medical clinics, the recreation center, and the detention center.

While not all YASU advisers had degrees in counseling, they brought something much more important to their job: an understanding of how to work with Vietnamese. In the United States, refugee service providers had learned that traditional Western approaches to mental health counseling generally fail with Vietnamese refugees. This is in part because of the stigma Vietnamese

"I was called to assist a Black Amerasian, Duoc, who had been beaten up by another Amerasian in a fight in school. When I met him in the clinic, he was angry, and I learned that he had been getting into a lot of trouble. I took him to my office and began talking to him. At first, he wouldn't talk, but I started asking him about where he was from in Vietnam. Luckily, he said that he was from Nha Do, an area in Vietnam where I was held as a political prisoner.

I told him that I had been there working in the prison camp when I saw a little Amerasian boy who was crying being led somewhere by an older Vietnamese man. Excitedly, he told me that he was that boy, and then he told me his story.

He said that he was abandoned by his mother in an orphanage. He was taken to live with a family 120 kilometers from Saigon in Dong Xoai for about five years. When the family could no longer afford to feed him, he was sold to a Communist cadre as a servant.

I realized I had seen him as he was being taken to his new 'home.' He said, 'I know you. I saw you working in the fields,' although I don't think he could possibly remember me among the many who were held there. However, he became very friendly towards me and called me his 'Daddy.' I told him that as my 'son' he had to stop getting into fights and stop being absent."

Pham Khuyen, YASU Adviser, January 1994

attach to mental illness and in part because the idea of sharing one's personal problems with a stranger is in conflict with Vietnamese notions of privacy and propriety (Carlin & Sokoloff, 1985; Tung, 1985). A report on the needs of Vietnamese students at a California university explains why Vietnamese students were not using the university counseling services: "[Vietnamese] students . . . will expect a more personal involvement [with the counselor], and usually will end up feeling alienated because they feel that they are being treated as a 'client,' rather than 'a special person' " (Ericksen & Cuceloglu, 1987, p. 59).

The advisers in the young adult program were effective because they provided the level of personal involvement that students expected. "They don't call me counselor or adviser. They call me uncle. They treat me like a member of the family," one adviser noted (Ranard & Pfleger, 1994). At the same time, advisers had to resist the temptation to solve students' problems for them—something that many students expected, but that would have been at odds with the overall program goal of helping students gain independence. "When they first come in, they want the adviser to solve their problems for them but we tell them that they are the ones to make the choices, not the adviser," an adviser noted. "We give information, offer options, and discuss consequences, but it's up to the student to take action" (Khuyen, personal communication, February 1994).

Conclusion

Through its experience with Amerasian young adults, the International Catholic Migration Commission learned several lessons about educating refugees. Perhaps the most important was that refugee education does not begin and end at the classroom door. Refugees in general and underschooled young adult refugees in particular have a wide range of needs, and to be effective a program cannot ignore students' psychosocial needs. The program could never have succeeded had it isolated educational needs from other needs, since the other needs so heavily affected students' ability to take advantage of the education offered.

A second lesson was that refugees know a great deal about what they need, and they should be heard. Of all the ways the program sought to give voice to students' needs, none was more effective than the use of bilingual Vietnamese-American advisers. They provided the program with a constant means of listening and responding to refugees.

A third lesson was that it pays to support experimentation. The International Catholic Migration Commission could respond to the special needs of Amerasians with a sophisticated array of innovative ideas and approaches, both inside and outside the classroom, because managers encouraged change and experimentation.

Counselor Pham Khuyen meets with a group of Amerasian young adults to discuss issues informally.

Few innovations would have occurred without organized linkages among the various social service agencies in the camp. This fact underscores the fourth and final lesson: the value of coordination and cooperation. The International Catholic Migration Commission, a large organization made up of many departments, was only one of many agencies operating at the processing center. In size and bureaucratic complexity, the center rivaled any midsized U.S. community, and as in any community, the different social service organizations were no strangers to competition and territorial disputes. Yet it quickly became clear to everyone that Amerasians' needs were so broad and involved so many different agencies that cooperation and coordination were imperative. This recognition led to better linkages that allowed staff to take full advantage of all the available resources and to provide students with the best educational experience possible.

References

Blundell, L. (1985, July 15). *The acculturation of Amerasian adolescents.* Unpublished report.

Carlin, J.E., & Sokoloff, B.Z. (1985). Mental health treatment issues for Southeast Asian children. In T.C. Owan (Ed.), *Southeast Asian mental health: Treatment, prevention, services, training, and research* (pp. 91-112). Washington, DC: National Institute of Mental Health.

Center for Applied Linguistics. (1988). *Young adult refugee survey.* Washington, DC: Author.

Cohon, J.D., Lucey, M., Paul, M., & Penning, J.L. (1986). *Preventive mental health in the ESL classroom: A handbook for teachers.* Providence, RI: American Council for Nationalities Service.

Ericksen, R.B., & Cuceloglu, D.M. (1987, October). *A report on needs assessment survey of Vietnamese students at California State University, Fullerton.* Fullerton, CA: California State University, Office of International Education and Exchange.

Felsman, J.K., Johnson, M.C., Frederick, T.L., & Felsman, I.C. (1989). *Vietnamese Amerasians: Practical implications of current research.* Washington, DC: U.S. Department of Health and Human Services, Office of Refugee Resettlement.

Gilzow, D.F. (1988). New focus on young adult refugees in the overseas program. *Passage: A Journal of Refugee Education, 4*(1&2), 44-46.

International Catholic Migration Commission. (1989). *Young adult services program: ICMC component of YASP.* Unpublished manuscript.

Kleinmann, H.H. (1982). External influences and their neutralization in second language acquisition: A look at adult Indochinese refugees. *TESOL Quarterly, 16*(2), 239-244.

Krashen, S.D., & Terrell, T.D. (1983). *The natural approach: Language acquisition in the classroom.* Elmsford, NY: Pergamon.

Ong, L. (1992). *Activity-based counseling and the adolescent Vietnamese refugees.* Unpublished manuscript.

Ranard, D.A., & Gilzow, D.F. (1989, June). The Amerasians. *In America: Perspectives on Refugee Resettlement, 4,* 3.

Ranard, D.A., & Pfleger, M. (1994). *Reflections on educating refugees: Interviews with staff of the overseas refugee training program.* Unpublished manuscript, Center for Applied Linguistics, Washington, DC.

Robinson, C. (1980). *Physical and emotional health care needs of Indochinese refugees.* Washington, DC: Indochinese Resource Action Center.

Ronk, D. (1986). The Amerasian child. *Passage: A Journal of Refugee Education, 2*(1), 32-35.

Schumann, F. (1980). Diary of a language learner: A further analysis. In R.C. Scarcella & S.D. Krashen (Eds.), *Research in second language acquisition.* Rowley, MA: Newbury House.

Snyder, S. (1990, March). *ESL literacy: What's working, why, and how?* Paper presented at the 24th annual convention of TESOL, San Francisco, CA.

Tung, T.M. (1985). Psychiatric care for Southeast Asians: How different is different? In T.C. Owan (Ed.), *Southeast Asian mental health: Treatment, prevention, services, training, and research* (pp. 5-40). Washington, DC: National Institute of Mental Health.

Wrigley, H.S., & Guth, G.J. (1992). *Bringing literacy to life: Issues and options in adult ESL literacy.* San Mateo, CA: Aguirre International.

Chapter Five
The World of the Past, the World of Tomorrow

Fred Ligon

The World of the Past, the World of Tomorrow

First Language Literacy at the Phanat Nikhom Refugee Camp

Fred Ligon
The Consortium
Phanat Nikhom Refugee Camp

It is 6:00 p.m. After a full day of English and cultural orientation classes, hundreds of students, mostly women accompanied by children, pack the dusty road on their way to yet another hour and fifteen minutes of instruction. The sounds of laughter and play fill the evening air as the students enter the classrooms.

Only a few visitors, or teaching staff for that matter, have ever witnessed this scene, yet it happens every weekday. The students are participants in a unique educational experiment: Phanat Nikhom's native language literacy (NLL) program. For five days a week, up to 1,800 students learn to read and write their own languages in classes taught by other U.S.-bound refugees, who, in some cases, are only recently literate themselves.

Established in 1982, the NLL program has provided literacy instruction to more than 30,000 Hmong, Mien, Lao, Lahu, Khmer, and Vietnamese refugees. The program was founded on the belief that refugees who can read and write their own languages will find it easier to learn a second language. The program also assumes that the skills refugees gain in NLL classes will contribute to their personal and cultural pride and that this pride in turn will help them face the challenges of adjusting to a new culture and language. Although for much of its history NLL has struggled for survival and acceptance, in recent years the program has flourished, in large measure because staff throughout the entire refugee education program at Phanat Nikhom have increasingly promoted bilingual communication rather than insisting on an English-only learning environment.

This chapter examines the role of NLL at Phanat Nikhom. The first part focuses on classroom instruction, while the second part explores efforts to expand the uses of native language literacy outside the classroom. Although the Consortium has provided literacy training to several refugee populations, this article will focus on the Hmong, since this group has played such an important part in the story of NLL at Phanat Nikhom.

Native Language Literacy Program

Early History

It was the Hmong and their interest in first language literacy that provided the impetus for the Consortium's first efforts in NLL instruction. The NLL program in Phanat Nikhom grew out of efforts begun 15 years ago in Ban Vinai, a camp for Hmong and Mien refugees on the Thailand–Laos border. NLL instruction in Ban Vinai began as part of a Ford Foundation–funded pilot program that provided six weeks of NLL instruction and ESL to adult hilltribe refugees who had been accepted for resettlement to the United States. Later that year, NLL and ESL classes in Ban Vinai became part of the overseas refugee program funded by the U.S. Department of State. Implemented by the Consortium, the new program continued to teach Hmong literacy, although the design differed from that of the first program: Whereas students in the Ford-funded program received NLL instruction at the same time they studied ESL, in the new program, students studied NLL before they began their ESL classes.

The continuation of NLL instruction was largely the result of efforts by Peter Loverde, a teacher trainer in the new program and a strong advocate for NLL instruction. While there was little research to support his views, Loverde believed that teaching refugee adults to read and write their own language would help them learn English. He and others in Ban Vinai also supported NLL as a means of linguistic and cultural survival for the Hmong. "Ban Vinai is the largest community of Hmong in the world," a 1981 Consortium report noted. "We should use this fact to keep alive the culture of the Hmong" (Consortium organizational memo HO 81-0325, December 1981). Hmong concern about cultural preservation has been well documented in the growing body of literature on this group (Dunnigan, 1986; Schein, 1987; Scott, 1982), and in Ban Vinai the NLL program generally received support from Hmong leadership. On one occasion, with tens of thousands of refugees relocated to Ban Vinai and space in great demand, Hmong leaders saw to it that the NLL program was allocated 20 to 30 classrooms (P. Loverde, personal communication, March 1994).

In early 1981, the training program at Ban Vinai moved to Phanat Nikhom. NLL did not survive the transfer, largely because Peter Loverde, NLL's strongest advocate, did not move to Phanat Nikhom at that time. In addition, there was less support for NLL instruction from the refugee community at Phanat Nikhom, where the refugees were more diverse in their ethnic and educational backgrounds than the largely nonliterate hilltribe community in Ban Vinai.

In mid-1981, Loverde rejoined the Consortium staff at Phanat Nikhom and almost immediately began advocating for an NLL program. His keen interest, coupled with the arrival in early 1982 of large numbers of hilltribe students, led to the establishment of NLL classes. The new NLL program returned to the Ford-funded model of simultaneous ESL and NLL instruction, with refugees studying English and cultural orientation during the day and NLL in the evening.

Obstacles

NLL instruction at Phanat Nikhom has survived despite many obstacles: initial resistance to NLL instruction from program funders, staff, and, on occasion, the refugee leadership; limited funding and resources; inexperienced volunteer teachers; and high refugee teacher turnover.

Most obstacles have derived from a widespread skepticism about NLL's benefits. NLL's struggle for recognition and acceptance began inside the Consortium among program staff. Some expressed concern that learning to read and write two languages—the students' own and English—would confuse the learners or hinder their learning English. Others questioned the relevance of NLL to the overseas training program's purpose—to prepare refugees for life in the United States.

From time to time, there was resistance to NLL from the refugees themselves. Hmong leaders, though generally supportive of NLL, at times also supported instruction in Lao, Thai, and English only. Refugees have also questioned the value of a particular writing system. Some Hmong have supported a different script from the one used in the NLL program, and one of the Mien scripts, developed in the 1930s by Western missionaries, has been controversial from the beginning because of its ties to Christianity.

Moreover, using U.S. tax dollars to support the teaching of any language other than English was politically sensitive, particularly in the program's early years. The program's State Department monitor, while sympathetic to the Consortium's efforts to re-introduce NLL instruction in Phanat Nikhom, was nonetheless acutely aware of the difficulty of justifying NLL to critics within the U.S. government. The overseas program was frequently under fire from critics who questioned the value of any pre-resettlement training. If critics thought an extensive pre-arrival English language program was unnecessary, one can only imagine their reaction to the notion of a native language literacy program.

For many Hmong refugees, one purpose for becoming literate in their own language is to be able to correspond with relatives in Laos.

The lack of research showing the benefits of native language literacy for English language acquisition in adult learners also made support for NLL instruction problematic. In hopes of shedding some light on the issue, the Asia Foundation funded a study in late 1980 to examine the effects of first language literacy on the ESL performance of Hmong students in the refugee program at Ban Vinai. The study found that literacy in Hmong had a positive effect on learners' ESL performance. The small sample size (64) and the short period of instruction, however, limited the significance of the findings (Robson, 1982).

Nonetheless, Loverde and others in Phanat Nikhom continued to advocate for NLL instruction, taking every opportunity to explain to staff and visitors its instructional benefits. Skeptical staff were gradually won over as they saw firsthand the enthusiasm of the refugees and the gains students were able to make (Ranard & Pfleger, 1994).

Because of the growing support for NLL among staff at Phanat Nikhom, and because the classes were taught by volunteer refugee teachers and made minimal demands on the budgetary resources of the overseas program, NLL classes were allowed to continue.

Educating Women

"I don't like it when a letter arrives. If my husband is not home, my children and I have to wait. We want to know what is written there."

As the sunlight breaks through the mist hanging loosely between the mountains of northern Laos, Mee Vang fixes breakfast for her children. Her husband is outside preparing to slaughter a chicken for the evening meal. The rice harvest will soon be in, and Mee Vang is working harder than usual on her *paj ntaub* embroidery to get clothes ready for the New Year celebration.

For Mee Vang, the rhythm of life was once marked by the rising and setting of the sun, the planting and harvesting of the crops, and the raising of animals. She produced everything she needed by hand. Her children learned as she once had, by listening and by watching the elders sew cloth, plant fields, and form tools from wood and metal. The older generation told each new generation traditional stories; there was no need to write or read them. Those learning another language did so working alongside or trading with visitors from other villages beyond the mountains. The whims of nature and the toil of hard work dictated the terms of their survival.

In Laos, Hmong men often travelled from village to village and to places far from the mountains; some became literate, though more often in Lao than in Hmong. Most women, in contrast, were homebound and not expected to be literate; their daily tasks did not require literacy.

For Hmong women, life in the refugee camps and in the United States brought new needs and opportunities. For the first time in history, large

Program Description

NLL students study an hour and fifteen minutes each evening, five days a week, in the same classrooms they study in during the day. Each room holds about 20 students. Resources are limited— a whiteboard and marking pen, paper, worksheets, and a few workbooks.

Nearly two thirds of the students are women. (Among Hmong, the percentage of women is even higher: approximately 80 percent.) The students' ages range from small children accompanying their parents to grandparents in their 60s and 70s. Mothers often bring their babies with them.

numbers of hilltribe women were given the opportunity to become literate. In Phanat Nikhom, the percentage of women attending NLL is approximately 80%, indicating the continued interest women have in becoming literate.

The reasons women have for becoming literate relate to their culture, their families, and the camp environment, as well as to their own perceptions of themselves. In March, 1994, a survey asked NLL students in Phanat Nikhom why they wanted to become literate. The great majority of the respondents—who were mostly women—said they wanted to be literate to correspond with relatives and friends. In addition, they said they wanted to become literate to:

• Read and write Hmong folktales, history and other cultural material.
• Help children maintain their ties to Hmong culture.
• Gain access to information printed in Hmong.
• Communicate with relatives and friends in Laos or in the West.
• Help other Hmong become literate.
• Become a community leader.
• Write about the Hmong in China.

Commenting on the motivation of women to become literate, former NLL supervisor Peter Loverde notes, "Literacy is giving women, especially hilltribe women, the communication tools for the first time in history to understand the world beyond their own immediate confines and is opening up new and unexpected opportunities for them in the United States."

A simple, informal native language literacy test, administered to all new students, places those with little or no literacy in the NLL program. NLL classes are not organized by any system of levels—beginning, intermediate, and advanced—but some movement between classes occurs once teachers are able to identify fast and slow learners. The NLL instructors are volunteer refugee teachers whose educational backgrounds vary widely. Few have had previous teaching experience.

Family Classes

A recent initiative has organized NLL classes into three strands: adult classes, children's classes, and family classes. Family classes build on a common practice: Parents have always brought their children with them because the camp's day care center does not operate in the evening. While the program once viewed the presence of children as an unfortunate necessity, family classes are now seen as a way to strengthen intergenerational interaction. "The idea is that the parents and children can support one another," notes former NLL supervisor Robert Horley (personal communication, March 1994). "It lets the parents know what the children are involved in when they go to school. And we hope it starts the idea that parents can get involved in their children's schooling—that they will want to help their children study and support them when they do their homework." An added benefit of family classes is that they allow children to see their parents as learners.

The program's decision to focus on intergenerational issues led NLL staff to view family classes more positively and to plan other intergenerational activities. Literacy activities that parents and children can do together at home are being developed, and for parents with little or no literacy, NLL staff are creating picture books that family members can use in class or at home to tell each other stories.

Refugees Teaching Refugees

From the inception of the NLL program, all classroom teachers have been refugees. Over the past 14 years, approximately 3,000 refugees have taught native language literacy in Phanat Nikhom, and, at any given time, about 100 refugees are teaching in the program.

NLL teachers are generally young, most in their early twenties. Many have grown up in Thai refugee camps, and few have had formal education other than what they received in the camps. The degree to which teachers are literate in their first language varies. Some became literate in Laos or attended literacy classes in Ban

The teachers of native language literacy are U.S.-bound refugees, some of whom are only recently literate themselves.

Vinai or other refugee camps. Others became literate only after coming to Phanat Nikhom and continue improving their own literacy skills as they teach.

The decision to hire refugee teachers was made for budgetary reasons, but the benefits of the decision soon became apparent. The NLL program discovered what a growing number of adult ESL educators now believe: Literacy instruction can be more effective when teachers and students share a culture and language (Auerbach, 1994; Gillespie, 1994; Podeschi, 1990). For students who have not experienced classroom learning before, the classroom can be alienating (Auerbach, 1994; Klassen, 1991). When teachers and students share a common language and culture, the classroom environment is more likely to be relaxed, comfortable, and nonthreatening. Teachers know how to encourage classroom participation without violating traditional values. Moreover, teachers who are only recently literate themselves serve as models for what students can achieve.

Most NLL teachers prefer to use a traditional, bottom-up approach to literacy instruction, one that moves systematically from smaller to larger units of language. In the early stages, there is an emphasis on phonics, although every attempt is made to use meaningful language. A class often begins with teachers offering a written example or demonstration; a period for student practice then follows. Typically a lesson includes handwriting practice, dictation, exercises, and games, such as concentration and bingo. The teachers encourage students to demonstrate their writing skills on the board.

Students also seem to prefer a traditional teacher-centered classroom. For nonliterate students, learning to read and write is doubly difficult. At the same time they are learning new skills, they are adjusting to an unfamiliar learning environment; most, after all, have never been in a classroom before. For these students, a teacher-directed approach is effective because it approximates the way they have learned in their own culture: Daughters learn the skills of embroidery by observing their mothers and practicing; the skills of farming are passed from father to son in the same way. Because the style of teaching and learning is familiar, students learn to read and write with more confidence and security. While the program's approach evolved from experience, other literacy educators have also noted a preference among Hmong learners for a traditional pedagogy. In a review of the literature on Hmong attitudes toward their ESL classes, Duffy (1993) found a widespread dissatisfaction with modern communicative approaches and a preference for traditional approaches. Hvitfeldt (1986), in an article on Hmong learning style preferences, notes that "in all areas of social life, Hmong adults exhibit a preference for structure which is imposed from the outside over that which must be individually constructed" (p. 73).

Teacher Training

NLL teachers receive training from a small corps of trainers who are Thai nationals fluent in the refugee languages. The goal of teacher training is to create independent teachers, able to evaluate the progress of their students and to take the steps needed to improve their students' learning.

Training is provided through formal daily training sessions as well as through observation and feedback. Formal training takes place one hour each day at noon, around a long table occupying most of the training room. Training mirrors somewhat the model-and-practice approach used by most teachers. A typical session might begin with the trainer addressing a topic such as writing common punctuation marks (period, comma, exclamation point, etc.). The trainer might then write the marks on the board and lead a group discussion comparing their use in Hmong and English. The session might end with the trainer assessing comprehension by writing Hmong punctuation marks on the board and asking teachers to come up to the board and explain the marks.

In addition to these sessions, trainers observe and give feedback on classroom teaching. Feedback tends to be informal and in group gatherings rather than in one-on-one sessions. Since NLL teacher trainers monitor up to 40 teachers a day, however, observation and feedback sessions are limited. The training helps refugee teachers develop awareness of themselves as teachers and confidence in their ability to teach. The teaching quality varies—some teachers excel while others struggle, but few lack enthusiasm for their work.

Materials

Materials development has always been an important part of the NLL program. Classes use both published material as well as material developed by staff. In the early years, Hmong classes used workbooks and primers developed in the United States; for the Mien, Lao, Khmer, Vietnamese, and Lahu classes, staff adapted materials and workbooks because they were not satisfied with what was available.

Staff in recent years have developed a broad range of high-interest reading materials, including folktales and traditional sayings, an almanac, dictionaries, literacy primers, and a student newsletter. A recent materials development initiative builds on students' curiosity about life in the United States. Refugees post questions on a resource-room bulletin board. Staff then send the questions by e-mail to refugees in the United States; their e-mail responses are posted on the bulletin board next to the questions.

Among the most useful staff-developed materials is the Literacy Health Manual. Each of the manual's ten chapters has a brief reading passage about health and child rearing, accompanied by reading and writing exercises and word problems incorporating basic numeracy skills. Each manual is bilingual in English and one of five languages—Hmong, Lao, Khmer, Vietnamese, or Mien—with the native language and English versions on facing pages. Because of the focus on child rearing, the manuals have been especially popular with women.

In order to help students make the transition from learning to read to reading to learn, the program has developed a sizeable collection of Hmong and Mien reading materials. The collection consists of published materials as well as material translated into the native languages by NLL staff at Phanat Nikhom. In the case of published Hmong works, for example, the amount of written material in the United States has expanded significantly in recent years, and the program's collection now includes folktales, novels, newspapers, newsletters, health bulletins, and bilingual driving examinations.

In addition, the program has translated other Mien and Hmong materials: mostly popular Western literature and math and science texts. The NLL staff decided to emphasize this type of material for two reasons. As noted earlier, quite a few Hmong folktales have already been published, and many of these are part of the program's collection of materials. More importantly, NLL staff members were concerned that an excessive focus on Hmong folktales and cultural stories might have the unintentional effect of freezing the written language in a time of the past, granting the Hmong a means of preserving their language and culture but allocating them few resources to expand their knowledge of the world in their own words. The new material, it was hoped, would help the Hmong realize that "reading and writing can open up a whole new world" (R. Horley, personal communication, March

The NLL program at Phanat Nikhom has acquired, developed, and translated hundreds of materials, ranging from children's books to science texts.

1994). The NLL program is also working on producing a Hmong dictionary.

In translating math, health, science, and academic texts, NLL teacher trainers have had to create a new Hmong vocabulary. While not all invented words will achieve universal acceptance by the Hmong, the effort shows the Hmong that their language has value and is as capable as other languages of conveying ideas. Says former NLL supervisor Robert Horley,

I feel the effort to expand Hmong vocabulary has succeeded. From what I have been able to hear about Hmong in the United States, they are more successful because they arrive there feeling more confident about their language. A few years ago I used to hear Hmong saying, "Oh, you can't say that in Hmong." I'm not hearing that as often now. Now, I find they'll say, "We can say that. Whatever we want to call it, that's what it is." (personal communication, March 1994)

To house its growing collection of materials, the NLL program established a Hilltribe Resource Center, where refugees can choose materials from a broad array of interest areas, both traditional and academic. Located in a small room adjacent to the NLL complex and run by volunteer refugee staff, the center is also a place where refugees can learn how to use a library.

Hmong Scripts

Although the Hmong are often described as a preliterate people, Hmong legends tell of a time when the Hmong had their own written language. Different stories explain the loss of the script; most are set in the late 19th century, when many Hmong, to escape attacks and persecution, fled China for Vietnam, Thailand, and Laos. According to one story,

> Two Hmong brother-kings led a group of soldiers south from their villages in China. The women and girl-babies stayed behind and the soldiers traveled with the boy-babies and the female servants. When they got halfway, the two brother-kings were captured and put to sleep so the Hmong soldiers couldn't find them. Only the brother-kings could understand and teach the letters that they carried with them from China. Only the brother-kings knew how to keep the letters and how to teach them; without them the soldiers didn't know what to do or where to go. The soldiers waited and waited for the brother-kings to return. The new leader didn't know what to do, so he said the soldiers should cook and eat the letters the brother-kings carried with them. This would put the knowledge right into their minds. They would see which person would get the idea of the letters. But after eating the letters, they still did not understand, and all the letters were lost. Then everyone just stayed there, doing the best they could.
>
> —Told to Gayle Morrison by Xao Ying Xiong, Santa Ana, California

Though many Hmong in the 20th century have been nonliterate, this can be attributed largely to their independence and isolation. In Laos, Hmong preferred to live in isolated mountain regions, high above the lands farmed by the Lao and other ethnic groups. Because of their isolation, many Hmong received no formal education.

Surprisingly, more than 20 Hmong writing systems have been developed in this century. Most, however, have gained little or no acceptance. Writing systems developed by missionaries mostly gained audiences equivalent to the size of their congregations, though this was not the case with the Romanized Popular Alphabet (RPA), the most commonly used written script.

Unlike most other Hmong writing systems, the RPA is easily produced on standard English language typewriters, keyboards, and printing presses. Consequently, materials written in Hmong RPA have proliferated, launching a literacy chain reaction: As more materials have become available in Hmong, more Hmong people have become interested in reading. The use of RPA in the 1970s and 1980s by Hmong in refugee camps in Thailand further solidified its position. In the past decade, RPA has seen even wider use as it has been adopted by Hmong in China corresponding with other Hmong around the world.

All materials developed by the Consortium are written in the RPA. Still, not all Hmong people accept the RPA as the only way of writing Hmong, and other writing systems have gained a measure of acceptance. Alternative Hmong writing systems continue to be developed by Hmong in the United States.

NLL Throughout the Consortium Program

Before leaving home for cultural orientation class, Kia Vue closely studies the paper her teenage son, Chue, brought home from school yesterday. It is an invitation to attend Open House at PASS, the Consortium's junior high school. Kia carries her baby to the preschool program, stopping to read a poster tacked on a wall. A meeting with parents is scheduled for Saturday to discuss the preschool snacks, something of concern to Kia and her husband. Outside her cultural orientation class, Kia pauses for a few minutes to look at pictures of dinosaurs on an outdoor bulletin board. As Kia reads the accompanying Hmong text, explaining the prehistoric animals, she is relieved to discover that dinosaurs no longer exist and won't be awaiting her in Minnesota. Later, in cultural orientation class, Kia's teacher passes out slips announcing registration for elective classes. Kia tells her teacher she will sign up for one on how to make puppets for her children.

Kia, a beginning-level ESL student who never studied in a classroom before coming to Phanat Nikhom, can read the school notice, the poster on the bulletin board, and the class registration announcement because they were written in Hmong, a language she has been studying for five months in her NLL class.

Each day Kia discovers many opportunities around Phanat Nikhom to apply her emerging Hmong literacy skills. These opportunities have not always existed. Although refugees have been studying NLL at Phanat Nikhom since 1981, until recently the program provided few chances for refugees to use their new skills outside NLL classes. To help prepare students for resettlement in the United States, the program made English the language of communication in Phanat Nikhom, and until 1991, virtually all written communication with refugees took place in English. Classroom rules, workplace signs and safety warnings, reporting forms, and even the student newsletter were all in English.

Yet this practice was not in harmony with other program goals and efforts. For students with little or no English, the practice frequently led to miscommunication and missed opportunities to participate in activities. In their ESL and cultural orientation classes, students were encouraged to preserve their culture, yet outside class there were few opportunities to use one of the most important aspects of their culture. Moreover, the English-only practice was at odds with one of the program's fundamental goals: to promote student independence, initiative, and self-esteem. In some ways, the practice may have actually contributed to dependency, with adult refugees often forced to rely on their more English-proficient children for information. With Hmong as a language of communication in the camp, refugees could rely on their own newly emerging literacy skills. Encouraging two options—English and Hmong—would increase refugees' chances for independence and self-reliance.

Uses of Native Language Literacy

Today, Hmong is increasingly used throughout the program at Phanat Nikhom as a way to communicate with students and as a way to develop newly emerging native language literacy skills. The following provides a selective overview of the uses of native language.

In the Consortium's high school and elementary programs, communication between the school and home now takes place in the native languages and English. A parent–student handbook in Hmong, Mien, and Lahu provides information on school services. Notices to students and their parents, invitations to school events, and written materials used at Parent–Teacher–Student Association meetings are provided to families in their native languages. Important information, particularly concerning students' safety, is also in the native language. For example, during orientation to the "ropes course," a physically demanding obstacle course, objectives are written in the native language.

Around the high school complex, bilingual notices appear on bulletin boards and office and classroom walls. Posters in Hmong

Fathers are encouraged to take an active role in their children's education.

and English announce upcoming events, bulletin boards display native language letters from relatives in the United States, and newspaper articles describe Hmong students' experiences in their new U.S. schools and communities.

By providing opportunities for native language use during the school day, the refugee program helps students strengthen their connection to the native culture. In the elementary school program, students study language arts in Hmong. Not only do students read folktales and other storybooks in Hmong, they also create their own native language reading books as class projects.

At the school's recreation center, students participate in essay writing contests. Entries written in the native language by high school students are judged by advanced-level students in the adult program. Winning essays are then posted for all to read.

At the recreation center, parents teach a variety of elective classes, such as cooking traditional foods and playing traditional instruments. In addition, students make holiday greeting cards using the native language and publish a bilingual student newsletter with student-written poems and stories, letters from resettled refugees, and profiles of refugees who have been successful in the United States.

In the school's resource room, students take charge of their own learning by checking out bilingual language lab materials. Bilingual scripts for stories on cassette tape and supplementary native language readings about American culture are popular among both elementary and high school students.

The adult program also offers opportunities for students to use the native language. During supermarket simulations, adults read and write shopping lists in the native language. In ESL classes, some teachers give students vocabulary lists written in English and the native language to help them prepare for reading activities. Teachers increasingly see the value of note-taking in the native language; many students write English words phonetically in the native language as an aid to pronunciation. Some teachers have students read aloud letters, written in the native language, that teachers have received from former students.

In work orientation classes, safety signs in Hmong are posted around the classrooms. In cultural orientation, students learn to read maps in the native language, and background information for many lessons is translated into the native language. Once in each instructional cycle, parents bring their children to class to read books in the native language and to learn how important it is to read to their children.

In special classes for young mothers, students receive native language health pamphlets and hand-outs to be shared with family members at home. Students also share information about their families and, in their native language, write out personal and family goals. Students create picture books with drawings of traditional events and activities. While some students tell their stories wholly through pictures, others supplement the pictures with the words they know. Students share and read these student-made books with one another.

At the resource center, notices on a bulletin board provide detailed information in the native language about American holidays and curriculum topics. Other bulletin boards encourage students to write out their questions about life in the United States in their native language or English; their questions are answered in the native language by resource center staff.

In special tutorial sessions, appointment slips are written in the native language. During their study sessions, students take notes in both English and the native language.

Even special education students have opportunities to use native language literacy. Deaf students receive a booklet in the native language on the care of hearing aids. Disabled students take home a booklet, translated into their native language, explaining American law and the disabled. All special education students receive a booklet in the native language about home safety to take home to their families.

Reflections on NLL

Today, there is growing support for NLL instruction among adult ESL educators. In a review of the literature, Gillespie (1994) notes that educators support NLL instruction for a variety of political, social, cultural, and linguistic reasons. At Phanat Nikhom, the emergence of NLL instruction and the explosion of NLL use throughout the organization has been based less on the literature—until recently, there was very little written on native language literacy for adults—and more on some common-sense assumptions and beliefs about NLL's value. The Consortium's 14-year experience in Phanat Nikhom suggests that these beliefs have been well founded and that there are indeed significant benefits to NLL. Specifically, the program has found the following to be true:

1. NLL aids in the acquisition of English. Strategies developed in learning to read and write a first language help refugees learn to read and write a second language. Moreover, once students have learned to read and write one language—their own—they are more confident that they can learn to read and write a second.

2. Native language literacy provides refugees with another source of information and knowledge about the world. Vietnamese, Lao, and Khmer refugees who have made the transition to literacy have access to a large body of literature, and the amount of literacy material available to the Hmong continues to grow. It is hoped that newly literate Lahu and Mien will add to what is available in their languages.

3. Native language literacy contributes to personal and cultural pride. Refugees gain self-confidence when they are able to express themselves in writing in their own language. As Giroux (1987) puts it, "To be literate . . . is to be present and active in the struggle for reclaiming one's voice, history, and future" (page 11).

Perhaps the best evidence of the value of the NLL program is the number of refugees whose lives it has changed. Of the more than 60,000 refugees who have studied at Phanat Nikhom since 1980, about half could not read or write their own language when they entered the program. Most have gained at least basic native language literacy during their brief stay at Phanat Nikhom. Some have achieved much more.

The World of the Past, the World of Tomorrow

Kia Vue rose and made her way to the podium to address her teachers and fellow students. A beginning-level Hmong student, Kia had been chosen to speak for her fellow students at their graduation ceremony. Speaking in Hmong, Kia talked about her experience sewing and selling paj ntaub, *Hmong embroidery, in the camp's handicraft stalls before entering the refugee program. After completing five months of study, she still made and sold* paj ntaub *in the stalls, but her life had changed. Now she could understand and talk to her foreign customers, she could read and write her name and some words in English, and most important, she could read and write her own language. Kia paused, then began to cry. Alone at first, she was soon joined by others who cried and then applauded Kia for what she had accomplished.*

Literacy's power for change should never be underestimated or taken for granted. Kia Vue's graduation speech lingers as a reminder that the ultimate success of the refugee program is measured by its ability to move learners further toward self-reliance, confident they have the skills and the resources to begin new lives yet not forget who they are.

References

Auerbach, E.R. (1994). Reexamining English only in the ESL classroom. *TESOL Quarterly, 27*(1), 9-32.

Duffy, J. (1993, March). *ESL and alienation: The Hmong of St. Orien.* Paper presented at the 27th annual convention of TESOL, Atlanta, GA.

Dunnigan, T. (1986). Processes of identity maintenance in Hmong society. In G.L. Hendricks, B.T. Downing, & A.S. Deinard (Eds.), *The Hmong in transition* (pp. 41-54). Staten Island, NY: Center for Migration Studies.

Gillespie, M.K. (1994). *Native language literacy instruction for adults: Patterns, issues, and promises.* Washington, DC: Center for Applied Linguistics, National Clearinghouse for ESL Literacy Education.

Giroux, H.A. (1987). Introduction. In P. Freire & D. Macedo, *Literacy: Reading the word and the world* (pp. 1-27). New York: Bergin & Garvey.

Hvitfeldt, C. (1986, Winter). Traditional culture, perceptual style, and learning: The classroom behavior of Hmong adults. *Adult Education Quarterly, 36*(2), 65-77.

Klassen, C. (1991). Obstacles to learning: The account of low-education Latin American adults. In B. Burnaby & A. Cummings (Eds.), *Sociopolitical aspects of ESL in Canada* (pp. 253-264). Toronto: Ontario Institute for Studies in Education.

Podeschi, R. (1990). Teaching their own: Minority challenges to mainstream institutions. In J.M. Ross-Gordon, L.G. Martin, & D.B. Briscoe (Eds.), *Serving culturally diverse populations* (pp. 55-65). San Francisco, CA: Jossey-Bass.

Ranard, D.A., & Pfleger, M. (1994). *Reflections on educating refugees: Interviews with staff of the overseas refugee training program.* Unpublished manuscript, Center for Applied Linguistics, Washington, DC.

Robson, B. (1982). Hmong literacy, formal education, and their effects on performance in an ESL class. In B. Downing & D. Olney (Eds.), *The Hmong in the west* (pp. 201-225). Minneapolis, MN: University of Minnesota.

Schein, L. (1987). Control of contrast: Lao-Hmong refugees in American contexts. In S. Morgan & E. Colsen (Eds.), *People in upheaval* (pp. 88-107). Staten Island, NY: Center for Migration Studies.

Scott, G.M. (1982). The Hmong refugee community in San Diego: Theoretical and practical implications of its continuing ethnic solidarity. *Anthropological Quarterly, 55*(3), 146-160.

Chapter Six
Enhancing the Flavor

Lauren Hoyt

Enhancing the Flavor

Winning Partnerships Between Home and School

Lauren Hoyt
World Relief Corporation
Philippine Refugee Processing Center

The effort we are making to include parents in our classroom affairs validates the positive partnership that can lead to students' success. We develop a spirit of shared responsibility that ensures a commonality of goals and makes us realize that many cooks do not spoil the broth, but rather enhance its flavor.

Victoria Garcia, PREP instructional supervisor

From 1987 to 1994, educators and refugee families involved in a program called Preparing Refugees for Elementary Programs (PREP) worked together to forge a partnership for educating refugee children. This chapter describes PREP's efforts to develop a collaborative model for involving families in their children's education. Integral to PREP's success was a shift from a traditional educator-directed program for parents to one in which family members became active participants in educating their children.

Preparing Refugees for Elementary Programs

PREP operated from 1987 to 1994 as part of the overseas refugee program in Bataan, Philippines. Run by the World Relief Corporation, PREP prepared refugee children for elementary schools in the United States. During its eight-year history, more than 12,000 Vietnamese, Laotian, and Cambodian students attended PREP. In its last few years, the student population was completely Vietnamese, reflecting campwide demographics.

PREP students attended classes four hours a day, five days a week, for 18 weeks, while older family members attended English and cultural orientation classes run by other agencies in the camp. PREP used a whole language approach. Students learned to read and write English through shared reading, language experience stories, and sustained silent reading. Children also learned English, as well as new subject matter, through math, social studies, and science activities. Teachers assessed students' progress through anecdotal records and portfolios of student work. Teachers, families, and students all worked together to gauge student progress through regular conferences.

PREP teachers were Filipinos in their mid-twenties from a variety of professional backgrounds. Some were experienced teachers, while others came from other technical fields. All were proficient in English and eager to learn the latest instructional methods. Teachers taught four hours a day and spent another two hours planning and evaluating their instruction in teams of five to eight teachers. Each team was guided by a supervisor, an experienced Filipino or American educator. Supervisors observed teachers in classrooms, assisted in lesson planning, encouraged professional development, evaluated the quality of instruction, and developed instructional goals.

Early Efforts in Family Involvement

PREP's early efforts in family involvement tended toward the traditional. These efforts focused on informing parents of their responsibilities to the school rather than on involving them in the classroom. Each 18-week term—or cycle, as a term of study was known—began with an orientation. Held in a large hall with PREP administrative and teaching staff seated in front, these sessions were one-way transfers of information from school to parent. For two hours, various speakers outlined the goals of the PREP program, school expectations and rules, the curriculum, and classroom routines. Afterward, parents met with teachers, who summarized the presentations and asked for questions. No children were allowed to attend these sessions.

In addition to orientation sessions, twice each cycle—in the seventh week and in the last week—PREP parents came to their children's classrooms to receive progress reports. During the one-on-one parent-teacher conference, the teacher read from a lengthy form evaluating the child's English and math skills, attitude, and behavior. The conference lasted only 15 minutes, allowing little or no time for questions. Even when there was time, parents deferred to the teacher's authority and rarely asked questions (Ranard & Pfleger, 1994).

Parents were also brought into the school setting for social and recreational activities. They watched their children compete in games and relay races on field day and present poems, skits, dances, and dramas during social hour. Parents rarely were involved in the planning of these events, however; for the most part, they were only spectators.

One family involvement activity was different—the practice of home visits. Home visits evolved naturally from teachers' interest in their students' culture and language. Teachers lived in dormitories in the refugee camp, and in the evenings they took walks through the refugee neighborhoods, where they were often invited into their students' living quarters. Relaxing with families over fragrant glasses of jasmine tea, teachers listened with interest to stories of escape and laughed at anecdotes of daily life, which occasionally included incidents from the classroom.

As teachers spent more time in refugee homes, they began to see the extent to which families supported their children's learning. Student work papered living quarters, and improvised blackboards featured English vocabulary lists. Home visits also provided opportunities for informal progress reports, as adults often asked how the children were doing.

In the refugee camp, families came in different configurations, teachers learned. A child's caregiver might be an older brother, an aunt, or even a friend. Even in two-parent families, it was often not the parent who was most directly involved in a child's education. As researchers have noted (Caplan, Whitmore, & Choy, 1989; Rumbaut & Ima, 1987), there is a cultural tradition among Southeast Asian families of working together for the collective good of the family; in education, this commonly takes the form, particularly among Vietnamese families, of older brothers and sisters guiding their younger siblings' education.

The structure of camp life also contributed to family and community involvement in children's education. Refugee housing, in blocklike buildings holding 10 to 12 families, was a place where family and friends shared child care, food preparation, washing, and other routine tasks; in this milieu, any number of people might help a child with homework. School buildings were located in the refugee neighborhoods, making them easy to visit, and parents, aunts, uncles, grandparents, and even neighbors got into the habit of dropping by PREP to see how children were doing. It was not uncommon to see younger brothers or sisters peeking through the louvered classroom windows at any time of the day or night when a school activity was taking place.

A close relationship between school and home was beneficial to both, teachers began to realize. Family involvement could make teachers' jobs easier both inside and outside the classroom. Regular communication with families could help teachers connect their lessons to their students' lives and interests. Families who felt a part of their children's education would be more likely to communicate concerns, make suggestions, volunteer, and help their children with homework assignments.

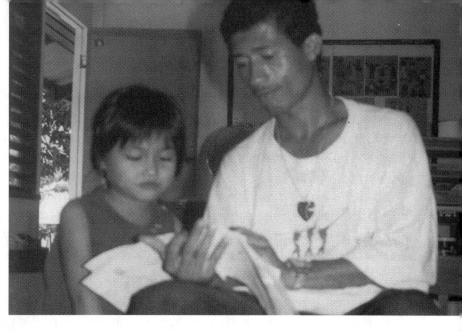

Southeast Asian parents want to participate in their children's education, but U.S. educators need to make a special effort to explain and encourage the kind of involvement they hope for.

Shift in Thinking

With the exception of home visits, PREP's early model for parent involvement paralleled practices at that time in the United States. PREP's top-down approach rarely elicited feedback from parents or involved them in planning educational activities; all worthwhile teaching was done by teachers, the program assumed. Parents were given information about school policies and practices and attended scheduled events, usually as passive spectators; if parents had concerns or questions of their own, it was assumed they would bring them to the teachers. There was little attempt to involve family members other than parents.

Gradually, a shift in perception and practice occurred, leading ultimately to a more collaborative model for family involvement. Home visits had shown teachers that family life offered rich opportunities for learning. As teachers began to view the home as a resource, they began to see family members as equal partners in the process of educating children. Teachers began inviting parents into the classroom to help teach; parents and other family members were encouraged to work on educational projects with children at home.

Getting family members actively involved, however, was not always easy. Among Southeast Asians, there was a cultural reluctance to assume a role that traditionally belonged to the teacher. In their own countries, family members might help repair school buildings or bring gifts to show their appreciation to teachers, but assisting with a lesson or teaching a game or song was considered the teacher's responsibility. Moreover, while well-educated parents might feel comfortable helping in the classroom, parents with little or no formal education often felt they lacked the necessary background to help their children learn.

If families were to become actively involved in their children's education, they would need encouragement and support. But what kind of support? To find out, staff began asking families what they needed to become more involved. Supervisor Victoria Garcia recalled (personal communication, March 1994), "When we asked parents to tell us how we could help them help their kids, they said, 'We need consistent help, we need to learn how to teach, and we need to be used in a way that really helps and that draws on what we know.' "

With a better sense of what families needed, staff developed strategies designed to improve school-home communication and more actively engage families. Among the most successful of these strategies were collaborative homework assignments, school visits, parent workshops, home–school journals, and parent–teacher associations.

Collaborative Homework Assignments

Most families indicated that helping children with homework was a high priority. To let families know how they could support what children were learning at school, staff developed homework letters. Translated into the native languages and sent home on a weekly basis, homework letters described the thematic unit for the week (e.g., food, families, animals, clothing), identified two to three instructional goals for that week, and provided suggestions for family homework activities. Homework assignments sometimes asked family members to share information about personal expe-

Parents who were reluctant to help in the classroom asked for training in how to work with their children more effectively.

riences and cultural values and traditions. Through these assignments, family members learned more about one another, and teachers learned more about individual family members' interests, experiences, and education, making it easier to involve them further in their children's education.

School Visits

Teachers encouraged parents to come to school and help their children present projects they had worked on together at home. Parents introduced themselves during "family week," helped their children cook traditional food during "food week," talked about their occupations during "community places and people week," helped their children prepare bulletin board displays on the weekly topic, and accompanied their children to the library to listen to stories and help them choose books. "It was nice to have parents in the classroom," recalled teacher Luz Bernaldez (personal communication, March 1994). "It developed a good relationship between the school and parents. Also, they could see development and improvement in their child's learning."

For family members with low levels of English and little formal education, it was essential to help preserve self-respect by allowing them to teach what they knew best. When students were learning about different occupations, for example, a parent who had been a farmer might come to school and talk about farming. Family members who didn't want to come to school, but still wanted to help their children learn, could work at home with suggestions from weekly homework letters.

Parent Workshops

Family members needed to participate in learning activities before they felt comfortable assisting teachers in the classroom or helping with homework. To provide families with a chance to experience typical school activities, such as shared reading with big books, and to see how games and songs were used to teach language, a team of teachers initiated parent workshops.

On six evenings throughout the 18-week cycle, families received training in activities related to positive learning attitudes and language acquisition. Family members were encouraged to talk about their own experiences as learners, describe ways in which they had successfully taught children at home, and ask questions they had about homework. Workshops were filled with spirited discussions on such topics as the benefits of praise and success in developing positive learning attitudes and the stages in learning to write. During the day, family members attended their own language classes, so it was easy for them to see parallels between their own learning and that of their children.

Home–School Journals

The idea for home–school journals grew out of staff's successful use of dialogue journals. Motivating reluctant writers to use their literacy skills for genuine communication, dialogue journals are written conversations between teacher and student (Peyton & Reed, 1990). Written in notebooks, these journals also serve as records of student progress. At PREP, dialogue journals brought children and teachers closer together and helped teachers incorporate information about the daily lives and interests of their students into their lessons.

Parent workshops introduce families to typical school activities, such as shared reading with big books.

With the permission of students, several teachers began sending journals home, asking family members to respond. These three-way conversations among teachers, students, and families provided non-threatening ways of seeking advice and sharing information. Teachers gained insight into their students' home lives, and family members became better informed about their children's education. For some, home–school journals were a way to discuss personal issues and feelings that they would not be willing to express otherwise. "Your compliments made me very happy," wrote the older brother of a student in a journal entry. "My father died in 1984. On behalf of my father, I tried to bring [my sister] along when I escaped from Vietnam and now bringing her up useful is the way that I'll render thanks to my parents."

Parent–Teacher Associations (PTAs)

Developed later in PREP, PTAs were initially proposed by teachers to bring families of individual classes together. Each class had its own PTA, electing a president and vice president to organize the association, facilitate meetings, and act as a liaison between families and classroom teachers. PTAs provided a forum for concerned family members to air frustrations and to come up with solutions to common problems. PTA meetings were a place where elders could reinforce traditional values and younger people could ask questions and develop leadership skills.

Because PTAs were organized by individual teachers, meetings varied in the ways they were conducted. In general, teachers found that when they facilitated meetings using English, parents participated less. Gradually, teachers learned to step back. They provided classroom space for associations to meet, organized meetings until officers were elected, and explained what kinds of help they needed for school events. After these initial meetings, parents often met on their own, communicating in their native language, bringing in teachers when they had questions or ideas to share. Through PTAs, parents developed leadership skills and their own support network. "Parents who knew each other from PTA helped support each other," teacher Emily Coinco recalled (personal communication, March 1994). "There were three families who weren't participating in home-school journal writing because the parents had not gone to school themselves in Vietnam and there were no older brothers or sisters at home to help. What happened was there were some highly literate parents in the neighborhood and in the PTA, and when they found out they sort of adopted these kids, tutoring them. That was one of the things I felt best about— that they began to help one another. It really didn't come from me; it came from them."

Thus, as teachers assumed less responsibility, families assumed more. Far from being passive, families came with distinct opinions about education, the role of teachers and schools in society, and the importance of education. They needed assistance in organizing meetings, a place in which to meet, and child care while the meetings took place. Once these were provided, the associations usually sustained themselves and grew.

Changes in Established Strategies

In addition to developing new strategies for family involvement, teachers began changing older, established ways of family involvement. Questionnaires designed to provide information about children's educational backgrounds and home life became more open-ended, fewer meetings were structured by teachers, and families organized themselves to mobilize volunteers to assist teachers in the classroom or with special events. Teachers spent less time talking and more time listening and observing. As teachers began to see families as rich sources of knowledge, they became more aware of families' educational interests and concerns and of family support networks and learning that were already in place in the home.

Parent-teacher orientation sessions evolved from school-wide formal meetings to more relaxed gatherings hosted by teachers in their classrooms. Families could see the inside of the classroom, begin to establish a rapport with the teacher, and meet other families. Many teachers postponed orientations from the first week to a later date and invited children to come with their families so that students could demonstrate classroom routines, sing songs, read books, and show parents their early work. Teachers felt that having children take part in the orientation was important. "Even if it was crowded, I wanted the children there. I wanted them to hear what I was telling their parents, so that they would know my expectations," teacher Rhodalyne Gallo noted (personal communication, March 1994). Personal contact with the entire family from the beginning underscored the value of families working together.

During home visits, teachers brought folders of student work and asked children to tell their families about what they had accomplished. Teachers asked families to help set goals for their child, to state their strengths and areas for concern, to help with their homework, and to give teachers feedback on classroom instruction. In their own homes, families were often willing to talk more openly with teachers.

Parent-teacher conferences also shifted toward a two-way flow of information rather than a teacher reviewing a lengthy report. Some teachers compiled short lists of questions that they sent home in English and the native language before each conference. In this way, families had time to think through responses and practice them in their new language. They had more self-confidence because they knew what would be discussed and they could prepare ahead of time.

What We Have Learned

Our experience with family involvement has taught us many lessons. Perhaps the most important of these is that, contrary to conventional wisdom, Southeast Asian refugee families *do* want to participate in their children's education. The type of participation U.S. schools hope for, however, will not happen by itself; it requires special effort on the part of educators. Here are some things that educators can do to promote family involvement:

1. Extend routine channels of communication. The school should take the initiative to contact families and develop personal relationships with refugee and immigrant families. To help staff better understand immigrant families' special concerns, schools can encourage families to form their own parent advisory boards. Home-school journals, homework letters, and home visits, done with the aid of translators if necessary, offer opportunities for families to express concerns and ask questions in a more relaxed atmosphere.

Educators need to understand that for many families, involvement in their children's education is a new concept that needs to be discussed, rather than mandated by institutions; other immigrant families can serve as models. Building trust and personal relationships requires an investment of time, but it is essential.

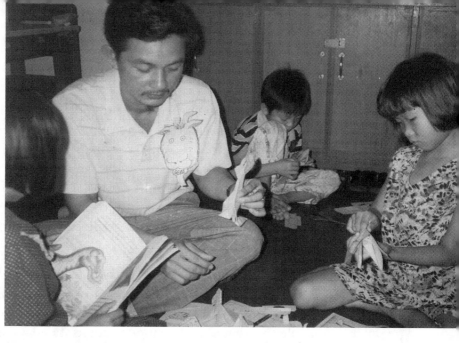

Children are able to follow classroom routines, sing songs, and read books to demonstrate accomplishments at parent-teacher orientations.

2. Explicitly explain classroom goals. In general, U.S. classrooms reflect methods of instruction that differ radically from those most Asian immigrants and refugees have experienced. In the typical Asian classroom, large numbers of students sit quietly in rows, responding only when directly addressed. Encountering the noisy activity of a U.S. classroom for the first time, many Asian parents wonder how children are able to learn. Therefore, teachers need to discuss different models of instruction and the expectations and roles of parents and teachers that these different models assume. Family members need to experience the kinds of instruction that they are asked to replicate. Older brothers and sisters should be actively recruited since they often serve as tutors and benefit equally from teaching (Caplan, Choy, & Whitmore, 1992; Rumbaut & Ima, 1987).

Home visits, homework letters, and videotaped examples of school activities or teaching methods can also reinforce information about school routines and instruction. These give access to vital information for those who cannot attend meetings at school. In the United States, many immigrant families own video cassette players; if teachers videotape workshops or classroom routines, children can provide a narrative at home.

3. Make the school environment newcomer-friendly. Educational institutions should be approachable and non-threatening. Institutions need to support alternative ways of working with families rather than assume that everyone deserves the same treatment or that families should learn to adapt to the norms of the dominant culture. With Asian immigrants, for example, communication may need to be negotiated through a neutral third party, especially when confronting problems.

Schools should look at their institutions through the eyes of the newcomer: Are translators available to explain expectations and school routines to new families? Are new families paired with established families so that school communications, holidays, and extracurricular activities are explained? Do families see a familiar face at school events? Are forms translated? When people walk into a school building or classroom, is work in the student's native language visible? Are there people in the school who are familiar enough with the families' culture to help avert situations that may be embarrassing, confusing, or insulting? An approachable, welcoming school environment is the product of awareness, forethought, and effort.

The school program should adapt to meet the needs of families, rather than expect families to adapt to existing structures. In public schools, this may mean separate PTA meetings or break-out discussion groups to allow for communication in native languages. Bilingual interpreters and translations of important documents should be provided. If finances allow, child care and transportation need to be provided so that everyone can participate. Personal invitations by teachers, community liaisons, or family volunteers also help assure adults that their presence at meetings is valued. Mothers, fathers, aunts, uncles, grandparents, brothers and sisters, and close family friends must be involved, since all are important teachers. Parent–teacher conferences may need to occur at home or on weekends when family members are available.

4. Make the process collaborative, with family members treated as full partners. Participation is rarely a problem when parents are encouraged to assume positions of responsibility—when they help plan, design, and assess activities, take leadership roles, and advocate for their children. Problems arise when time is not taken on a regular basis to check that educational programs are keeping pace with the needs and demands of the people they serve. Educators may need to give up their leadership roles and allow family members to set agendas and conduct meetings. Families need safe environments to ask questions, vent frustrations, discuss issues of importance to them, and learn ways of negotiating unfamiliar systems.

With a collaborative model, the educator becomes a facilitator who helps family members learn ways of interacting with school staff that are culturally appropriate for them and yet effective within the mainstream school culture. Teachers can act as liaisons between families and school, informing institutions of social and personal issues raised by students or their families.

5. Work within the community, involving mutual assistance associations and established social service organizations. In a 1994 survey of immigrants, refugees, social service providers, lawyers, and policy makers conducted by the National Coalition of Advocates for Students, respondents cited the need for school-community partnerships. According to Vivian Wai-Fun Lee (1994), "Increasingly, more schools realize that they alone cannot serve immigrant families effectively and that they need more bilingual and bicultural services. Schools are still not granting access to immigrant community-based organizations who want to provide services to immigrant schools at school sites. Many teachers are not aware of both pre-entry and post-entry trauma (i.e., poverty, prejudice, discrimination) experienced by immigrant families, which can be a hindrance to their children's learning."

Conclusion

In its last years of operation, PREP underwent a fundamental shift in the way its staff approached family involvement. Viewing families as resources, as "funds of knowledge" (González et al., 1993), PREP's shift in approach helped family members learn new skills, strengthened intergenerational ties, improved home-school communication, and helped participants achieve a sense of personal power and satisfaction.

As an institution, PREP underwent structural changes to keep pace with educators' interests. Budgets were redesigned, and new activities were supported. If only one teacher on a team wanted to experiment with a new approach, that teacher was given logistical support, time, and encouragement. Throughout the process, it was important that change was not mandated by program administrators, but rather came from teachers and families.

During PREP graduation ceremonies, parents, standing with their children, received recognition for their accomplishments as educators in their own right. At his children's graduation ceremony, a soft-spoken father of four and president of the PTA spoke enthusiastically of his experience as a PREP parent. "I find if I ask questions about my children's education, I can help them more," he said. "I want to know what they are learning. Having this opportunity here to be PTA president has really helped to inform me and give me confidence. When I go to America I will do the same—that is, get involved in my children's education."

References

Caplan, N., Choy, M.H., & Whitmore, J.K. (1992, February). Indochinese refugee families and academic achievement. *Scientific American, 266*(2), 36-42.

Caplan, N., Whitmore, J.K., & Choy, M.H. (1989). *The boat people and achievement in America.* Ann Arbor, MI: The University of Michigan Press.

González, N., Moll, L.C., Floyd-Tenery, M., Rivera, A., Rendon, P., Gonzales, R., & Amanti, C. (1993). *Teacher research on funds of knowledge: Learning from households.* Santa Cruz, CA and Washington, DC: The National Center for Research on Cultural Diversity and Second Language Learning.

Lee, V.W. (1994). *New groups and new challenges.* Paper presented at the Illinois State Conference for Teachers of Linguistically and Culturally Diverse Students, Chicago, IL.

Peyton, J.K., & Reed, L. (1990). *Dialogue journal writing with nonnative speakers: A handbook for teachers.* Alexandria, VA: Teachers of English to Speakers of Other Languages.

Ranard, D.A., & Pfleger, M. (1994). *Reflections on educating refugees: Interviews with staff of the overseas refugee training program.* Unpublished manuscript, Center for Applied Linguistics, Washington, DC.

Rumbaut, R., & Ima, K. (1987). *The adaptation of Southeast Asian refugee youth: A comparative study.* Washington, DC: U.S. Government Printing Office.

Other LIE Titles Available from Delta Systems

The following are other titles in the *Language in Education* series published by the Center for Applied Linguistics and Delta Systems Co., Inc.

Adult Biliteracy in the United States (ISBN 0-937354-83-X)
edited by David Spener

Approaches to Adult ESL Literacy Instruction (ISBN 0-937354-82-1)
edited by JoAnn Crandall and Joy Kreeft Peyton

Assessing Success in Family Literacy Projects (ISBN 0-937354-85-6)
edited by Daniel D. Holt

Cooperative Learning: A Response to Linguistic and Cultural Diversity (ISBN 0-937354-81-3)
edited by Daniel D. Holt

Immigrant Learners and Their Families: Literacy to Connect the Generations (ISBN 0-93-7354-84-8)
edited by Gail Weinstein-Shr and Elizabeth Quintero

Making Meaning, Making Change: Participatory Curriculum Development for Adult ESL Literacy (ISBN 0-937354-79-1)
by Elsa Roberts Auerbach

Speaking of Language: An International Guide to Language Service Organizations (ISBN 0-937354-80-5)
edited by Paula Conru, Vickie Lewelling, and Whitney Stewart

Talking Shop: A Curriculum Sourcebook for Participatory Adult ESL (ISBN 0-937354-78-3)
by Andrea Nash, Ann Cason, Madeline Rhum, Loren McGrail, and Rosario Gomez-Sanford

To order any of these titles, call Delta Systems, Co., Inc. at (800) 323-8270 or (815) 363-3582 (9–5 EST) or write to them at 1400 Miller Parkway, McHenry IL 60050.